Landesman's Journal

Meditations of a Forest Philosopher

LANDESMAN'S JOURNAL

Meditations of a Forest Philosopher

by

Richard Schain

Paragon House
Saint Paul

First Edition 2016

Published in the United States by
Paragon House
3600 Labore Road
St. Paul, Minnesota

www.ParagonHouse.com

Library of Congress Cataloging-in-Publication Data

Names: Schain, Richard J., author.
Title: Landesman's journal : meditations of a forest philosopher / by Richard Schain.
Description: First [edition]. | St. Paul : Paragon House, 2016.
Identifiers: LCCN 2015050212| ISBN 9781557789228 (pbk. : alk. paper) | ISBN 9781610831024 (e-book)
Subjects: LCSH: Soul--Miscellanea. | Ontology--Miscellanea. | Metaphysics--Miscellanea.
Classification: LCC BD423 .S33 2016 | DDC 191--dc23 LC record available at https://lccn.loc.gov/2015050212

Manufactured in the United States of America

10 9 8 7 6 5 4 3 2 1

The paper used in this publication meets the minimum requirements of American National Standard for Information Sciences—Permanence of Paper for Printed Library Materials, ANSIZ39.48-1984.

Dedicated to
those who tend their soul

ACKNOWLEDGMENTS

On the advice of Paragon House, I have added a biobibliography index of the writers and philosophers mentioned in this work, and their relevant writings. Finally, I acknowledge my gratitude to my wife Melanie Dreisbach for the indispensable role she has played in preparing this manuscript for publication.

INTRODUCTION

I FIRST MET Leon Landesman while I was walking my dogs in a remote corner of the mountain forests of south central Arizona. It was near the Mexican border, but how close I could not say. Landesman was with his own dog, a fierce-looking mongrel that growled aggressively at my own two large but good-natured Rhodesian Ridgebacks. He was an erect, well-built man, of medium height, with a thick covering of white hair and a Trotsky-like, grayish beard. He looked as though he might have been anywhere from fifty to seventy years of age. Later I learned he was in his mid-seventies when we first met. He said nothing when we tried to keep our dogs from a dustup but later he became a bit friendlier, revealing a slight Russian-Jewish accent.

As most dog owners do, we engaged in casual conversation. I learned that he lived in a small cabin, quite close to the border and only a few miles from my home. He had been there alone for a long time. As our conversation deepened, I found that we had a similar ancestry, originating from the former city of Ekaterinoslav in the Czarist Ukraine, now Dnepropetrovsk. This may have accounted for how we became intimate so quickly. We were *Landsmanner*, a word that also was Leon's surname. I was surprised to learn that this forest hermit had strong literary and philosophical interests, and read French, German, and Russian. What surprised me the most, however, was that he owned and had read some of my own books, a discovery that was a rare experience for me. We soon became fast friends and I would often visit his cabin where we drank Absolut Vodka and exchanged confidences about each other in the intimate Russian style.

Landesman had been an orphan in Russia; he was raised by a childless Jewish couple who brought him to the United States in 1930 when he was five years of age. Following a stint in the Army during World War II, he had attended the City College of New York; then graduate school in philosophy at New York University, hearing lectures from many luminaries in philosophy. I don't know all the details of his life, but at a certain point he unexpectedly obtained a job with the U.S. Post Office in southern Arizona. After a few shot glasses of vodka, he confided to me that he had been married twice (which surprised me) but each marriage had apparently ended without offspring. Later, I learned much more about him from his journal.

When I met Leon, he was a virtual recluse, without relatives and apparently with only one friend—a Mexican marijuana smuggler named Gustavo who crossed the border periodically and slept in Leon's cabin. He asked me not to spread this information about, saying he didn't want to have problems with the Border Patrol. Leon himself did not look upon Gustavo's occupation unfavorably since he was a pronounced libertarian and felt his friend had no other way of supporting his family. Landesman himself did not indulge in drugs as far as I could tell. He did, however, sip vodka at all hours of the day. He only drank the quality brand from Sweden that he insisted would not adversely affect his health. I never saw Leon obviously intoxicated at any time.

The one striking feature of Leon Landesman was his voracious reading habits. Almost all the wall space of his abode was covered with bookshelves; besides the books shelved, there were piles of them everywhere on the floors. He told me good-humoredly that he wished he had a library where he could arrange them, but he was fatalistic. "The goddesses of fate do not wish me to have a library," he said smiling. "They have favored me in many other ways so I have no cause for complaint."

* * *

Circumstances brought me to Paris for several months. When I returned, I brought back the French translation of Franz Rosenzweig's *Star of Redemption* that I knew he had been desirous of obtaining. As soon as I was able, I walked the few miles from my house to Leon's cabin to present him with my find. Ominously, the cabin door was boarded up and there was no sign of Leon or his dog. I was able to enter through a window and found Leon's home in a state of utter chaos. His books and boxes of typed papers in manuscript format were disorganized and scattered all about. The little kitchen was a mess, having obviously been visited by wildlife in the area. I had a foreboding that my friend was no longer in this world.

Later I drove to the Border Patrol office and found out what had happened. He was found dead in the cabin by a patrolling officer who heard his dog barking continuously. No autopsy was performed since he was elderly and it was presumed he had died of natural causes. There was nothing of consequence in the cabin except his books, some scattered manuscripts, and a few personal possessions. Arrangements had been made to donate the books to the county library but nothing had been done yet. No will or letter or anything directing what should be done after his death had been found. An expected ending, the clerk in the Border Patrol office told me, for a man who had lived such a bizarre life.

The whole thing was quite depressing for me. I had been more attached to Leon than I had realized. His life and death seemed so meaningless, given his intellectual capacities. Some time afterwards I went to the Post Office to pick up my mail. To my surprise, there was a thick packet there addressed to me from Leon. When I opened it, I found a single-spaced manuscript of over one hundred pages. I recognized the script as originating from Leon's ancient word processor. He must have mailed it to me shortly before his death. There was no note, only the manuscript. I brought it home, and after some hesitation, began to read it.

It was an amazing experience for me to read Leon's manuscript. A side of him emerged of which I had been totally unaware. Leon had had the mind of a philosopher with a remarkable capacity for self-expression. What was most amazing to me was the similarity between my own writings and his manuscript. Leon obviously had read my books with care and understanding—something he had given no indication of to me while he was alive. However, I had to admit to myself after reading the entire manuscript that Leon had gone far beyond my own work. There was an audacity and originality to his thoughts that I have never achieved. Writing in the format of a journal, he was able to avoid the heaviness and pedantry of most philosophical writings. His style reminded me of Amiel or Pessoa's *Book of Discontent*. Some uncharitable reader might see it as a prose analogue to Allen Ginsberg's *Howl.* There was nothing of the contemporary philosophical esotericism; he was a *lightfooted* philosopher, the type Nietzsche had recommended for philosophy but who is rarely found. I could see the depth, intensity, and fluency of his writing steadily increasing as the journal progressed, suggesting that this was a new form of expression for him even though he must have been already in his seventies when he began the journal. At times, I wondered if he was in some mysterious way an *alter ego* of mine.

Landesman's principal subject is the human soul, especially his own soul. He inveighs against the current habit of regarding the idea of the soul as a dead letter or a superstition irrelevant to modern life. Over and over, he emphasizes his reasons for believing that attending to one's soul is the most important part of the human condition. He defines and describes his concept of the nature of the soul and goes into detail about how one's soul develops. Writing is one of the most important ways in which

Landesman develops his own soul and is the justification for the time he puts into this activity. Readers are of little importance to him. Dogmatic religions and one-dimensional scientism are the two main barriers in his view to spiritual development.

Up to this point, many readers will be sympathetic to Landesman's views. But then he develops more radical ideas in dealing with the question of "God." For him, God is a necessary reality, but Landesman's God is not God the Father, but an Elder Brother working in a common enterprise. God is not an all-powerful and all-knowing Supreme Being. Rather, He is dependent on human souls for his own development and ability to flourish. The important point is that the dependency is mutual, not one-sided. Other points are made that a reader will have to discover for himself. He quotes with approval from the seventeenth century mystical poet-philosopher Angelus Silesius. The quotation is in German (segment 47) and since few English readers will be able to decipher it, I will give a purely literal translation:

I know that God cannot live one instant without me,
If I should come to naught, he must cease to be.

It is clear that Landesman himself is a mystic through and through, a label that he does not reject. His ideas are highly intuitive rather than strictly logical.

Landesman's style is personal, and in this also he is like Nietzsche. One might paraphrase Walt Whitman by saying he who touches this book touches a philosopher. He is intimately involved in his own mind with many of the important figures of Western thought. If one had to categorize his philosophical form, it might be called *existential* although this term has become an almost meaningless cliché. However, I cannot think of a better one to describe Landesman's writing.

* * *

I don't know if Leon ever seriously attempted to publish anything, philosophical or otherwise. The contact with literary agents that he mentions seems to have been uniformly unsuccessful. He certainly had no academic or literary credentials to serve as a platform for his work. His *Journal* is not a systematic treatise or a masterpiece of literary prose. At times, it seems to me to verge on incoherence. Nevertheless, Leon Landesman had ideas of great importance and originality. In a world concentrating solely on the surface of things, they ought to be read by a larger readership than myself alone. I am not aware of any extant family of his that could take responsibility for preserving his writings; thus I feel the responsibility to do so falls upon me.

The manuscript ends abruptly, perhaps because of the onset of some physical or mental infirmity. It could not have been sudden death because Landesman was capable of placing the manuscript in a large envelope, addressing it and mailing it to me. However, I did note the address was written with a markedly tremulous hand as if his nervous system were not functioning properly.

The entries in the manuscript are dated only with an abbreviation of a month, without day or year. I have substituted numbers for these abbreviations for the sake of clarity for later reference. One can only speculate as to the years of the composition of this writing. There are repetitions and contradictory statements as might be expected in any journal. It was not titled; the heading *Landesman's Journal* and the subtitle are my own additions. Most of the printing was done on the reverse side of pages that had been used for other purposes; perhaps earlier writings to which he makes reference, but no other full manuscripts have yet been found in the cabin. These earlier writings had lines drawn through them so that it was clear which was the current side. But Landesman in general had no sense of an orderly maintenance of his literary work. He probably had burned in his stove much of which he had written in former years. Rare editorial comments of mine regarding this manuscript are enclosed in brackets.

* * *

There is a tragic quality to the life of Leon Landesman. Circumstances and his peculiar temperament led him to live apart from American society. His way of life was suited for very few people. Perhaps, like the Socrates reported by Xenophon, he had come to feel that it was time for him to "pass on." Now that death has conferred its special distinction upon him, it may be proper for the public to become aware of an individual who had lived, thought, and expressed himself in a unique manner within its midst. He had ideas to communicate that deserve attention. But *attrape qui peut,* as Landesman says early in his *Journal.*

LANDESMAN'S JOURNAL

1

When I leave my subjective world and try to look at myself in an objective manner, it might be considered as a bizarre picture. I have been writing philosophy according to my own lights for many years and yet I have acquired hardly more than a dozen readers, if that many. Anyone passing judgment on my work would have to conclude that it is the scribbling of an eccentric, written only to satisfy his own egomania to no real purpose. Given this likely judgment, why do I persist in a meaningless effort? On occasion, I have created intellectual "spins" to justify myself but these are probably all rationalizations. The truth is that I don't know why I continue to write philosophy. The unpleasant metaphor occurs to me that it is akin to the visceral activity of intestines producing fecal manner. There may be some significance to this activity; but what it is, I have not the slightest clue. The writings are like long ditties that I croon to myself. If there is a more profound explanation of my writing activity, someone else will have to arrive at it.

2

The *creation of my inner self*—this is the key to my writing and the only intelligent response to the above entry. Writing has made me what I am. Other readers are irrelevant to this process.

* * *

Among the sayings of Jesus, one of the greatest was when at the end of his last Passover he encouraged his disciples saying, "Be of good cheer, I have overcome the world" (John 16:33). This saying seems to me to be of great significance. For us ordinary mortals, that is not easy to do. The world is strong and we are weak. But our souls depend upon accomplishing it.

3

I have prepared two manuscripts in the past three years [these have not yet been discovered—Ed.] and am en route to a third. The well is now dry and no more will be forthcoming for a long time, perhaps never, considering my age. I have had my say, done my duty to myself, materialized what is within me and left it to the great unknown of the future. Now I can sit back and relax with a good conscience. As far as the fate of my writings is concerned, I can say with Alfred de Vigny, "*attrape qui peut.*"

4

The importance of metaphysics is the basic theme of all my writings. If there is no reality to my soul, then all my writings have been for naught—merely a childish building of castles in the sand: here today, gone tomorrow. I don't claim that I have perceived the risen Christ or anything of a similar nature; I only report what I have clearly experienced within myself. I have experienced metaphysical realities as distinct from material realities. It is impossible for me to deny the importance of these experiences.

The experience of realities manifests itself in consciousness, which is clearly a metaphysical phenomenon. Language is the tool I use to describe and define for myself experiences of reality. I am only able to describe and define what has entered into my consciousness; thus metaphysics forms the basis of my writing activity.

The personification of the ultimate metaphysical reality has been named "God," or its equivalent in the languages of the Western world. The Christian Trinity is an (unsatisfactory to me) elaboration of this name. Jehovah, Adonai, The Holy Spirit, the Oversoul (Emerson), Brahman, Allah are all different names that have been applied to this ultimate reality, arising from different viewpoints. While the concept of a uniquely divine man called Jesus Christ who walked the earth lends a concrete aspect to this kind of metaphysical thinking, a specific event should not be given universal meaning to the exclusion of any other events of a similar nature.

5

Nicholas Berdyaev, the twentieth century philosopher to whom I look toward most for inspiration, wrote too much, especially in his last years. He desired too much to communicate his vision to the world. Sometimes he lapses into absurd cosmic ruminations. To what end? No one now pays attention to him (except perhaps me and a few other devotees). He would have done better to try to write about himself instead of thinking about "humanity."

The *Realm of Spirit and the Realm of Caesar*, his last published book, was an attempt to be more modest in his goals. The idea of Christianity as the hope of mankind is abandoned; Christ is barely mentioned. The writing is less frenetic, more measured, as befits a great sage. It is appropriate that this was his final writing.

6

I am rereading Berdyaev's books, which are a continuing source of strength to me. He is the philosopher of freedom of the spirit *par excellence.* However, the one thing about him that gives rise to my irritation and even at times to suspicion is his persistent endorsement of Christianity and incorporation of Christian dogma into his own ideology. I don't know why he cannot see Jesus as a great Jewish prophet, no more God-like than other great human figures. He puts forth his Resurrection as an example of metaphysical reality. To me, it is all just idol worship and makes me realize that N.B. had his limitations.

* * *

It is evident that my emotional state does not keep up with my philosophical development. Snide remarks about my writings still bother me. I must make my sensitivities conform to my intellect. If I am a genuine spiritual microcosm, I must learn to play the role fully: to *become* the role.

7

Whenever I have a guest for any length of time, it takes days for me to recover my mental equilibrium. I have nothing in common with the few people I know, so their presence requires a continual effort of adjustment on my part. This is just part of a more general problem I have of being unable to connect with my social milieu. No one I know shares my metaphysical or philosophical interests and I care nothing for the usual items of American discussion: politics, sports, golf, home repair, and the like. The things they are interested in have no interest for me. Hence I am a psychological isolate. (I cannot imagine my misery if by some quirk of fate I ever obtained celebrity status.)

But some consequences of psychological isolation are not good, to say the least, and I often feel depressed. I constantly wonder about the purpose of my existence and whether I should be doing something different with my life. I don't think this brooding would occur if I fit into a congenial personal milieu. But this is not the case, so I must make the best of my situation. Always I fall back on myself, my own *soul*, which I try to develop and strengthen to the best of my ability. I have faith that there is a larger metaphysical significance to my soul beyond my own particular circumstances.

Recently, I have ordered three books by Lev Shestov, a Russian-Jewish metaphysical philosopher. He is a "*landsman*" of mine, if I may utilize a Yiddish term. Hopefully, I will learn something from him. *Man darf lernen*—one has to learn—as my father often said. It is a necessity for one's soul.

8

I notice that the literary agents who have rejected my most recent writing are virtually all women (girls?). My impression of them from their websites and the responses is that they would be better suited as boutique or salon managers than as literary people. They seem very practical, personable, conscious of appearances, and business oriented. But for them to decide about philosophical merit—I think not! (To do these ladies justice, they invariably say they are not the right person for my work, which is, of course, quite correct.)

Vasily Grossman in *Life and Fate*, the English title of the long Russian novel of World War II, says how hard it is to be an "orphan" of the times—to be unloved by one's society. This novel has been compared to Tolstoy's *War and Peace* so I think Grossman's thought should be taken seriously. He could be talking about the orphan philosopher Leon Landesman.

9

I am still penetrating the philosophical writings of Lev Shestov. His style seems to me to be a mixture of Heine and Nietzsche but with his own special humanistic worldview. He is said to be a Russian Jew but there is nothing Jewish about his writings. Shestov is the most *original* and *interesting* writer I have come across in a long time. Like Berdyaev (of whom he was a lifelong friend), I wish I could read him in his native Russian.

My conception of a philosopher is analogous to the solitary eagle soaring high in the skies and who acquires metaphysical consciousness through experiences and readings, but most importantly through his own thoughts, intuitions, and visions. Like the high-flying eagle, his principal characteristic is *solitariness.* Not for him are the feeding dumps of university "philosophers" who roost together in academic guilds. Soaring high is the type of philosophic existence toward which I have always aspired.

10

I can no longer function effectively in my surrounding society. I anger easily because I am aware of my limitations. Those with whom I occasionally come in contact have no confidence in my abilities and they are right. I must learn to give over decisions and activities to other people more adapted to society.

The one area where my capacity has increased rather than diminished is my interior self. Here I am on an upward trend. Here is where I must put those energies that are left to me. Old age with its steadily diminishing supply of energy has crept up and I must deal with it appropriately.

In spite of my age, I would like to be able to learn to read Russian. Reading Berdyaev, Soloviev, Dostoevsky, Shestov, and the like would greatly enhance my tired brain and refresh my yearning soul.

11

Shestov says progress does not lie in the line of time but in a line perpendicular to it whose base is the human personality. Thus, development of the individual is the only genuine form of progress (*Penultimate Words, I*). This thought sums up my entire philosophy. In order for societal progress to occur, the individual must be free. Not only free from physical constraints, but also from the psychological constraints that are far more common within the world of today. Our stability-obsessed society uses psychology for mind control; thus progress of the individual means self-emancipation from the myriad of psychological pressures that are set up as guides for the individual. I don't have to enumerate the societal "values" established as goals for *Homo sapiens* or go into these values, as every thoughtful person will know what they are.

* * *

"Progress is perpendicular to the timeline" (Shestov)—a saying to be reflected on.

* * *

Russia under the Czars produced a special brand of spiritual writers and philosophers—e.g. Tolstoy, Dostoevsky, Soloviev, Shestov, Berdyaev, and no doubt others with whom I am not familiar. But 70 years of Communist rule may have destroyed this precious growth of human culture. Let us hope that, like the phoenix, Russian spiritual culture will rise again!

12

Rereading N.B.'s *Spirit and Reality*. I greatly admire Berdyaev's conviction about "theandrism" and search my own soul for evidence of a God connection, but can find none. God as a spirit seems to want nothing to do with me. Perhaps because I have a Jewish ancestry he avoids me, since my forebears were supposedly the cause of his son's crucifixion. There is nothing I can do about that. But de Vigny felt the same even though he was not Jewish.

* * *

Today I completed *Existential Philosophy of the Spirit*. It is certainly my swan song for an extended piece of writing, although I have thought this before. But I really have nothing further to say in a philosophical mode. Also, having been raised in the era of typewriters, I can no longer contend with the computer skills required of a writer in today's age. I am comfortable with my obsolete Smith Corona, but can progress no further with mechanical writing machines. It comforts me to know Nietzsche could not even use a typewriter to overcome his illegible handwriting.

13

I have come to believe that the principal purpose of philosophy is to bring the reality of metaphysical being into one's consciousness. People are divided into two groups—those who are aware of metaphysical reality and those who are not. The latter are far more numerous in the science-dominated world of today, which is why most people are so uncongenial to me.

I think those whose minds are occupied with metaphysical reality are more likely to survive death than others. I am convinced that in some form or another, my soul will survive the death of my material body. The more I immerse myself in metaphysical realities that are the nutrients of the soul, the more alive my soul will be after death. This thought of mine is not subject to rational proof, deriving as it does from intuitive feelings. In any case, it has dissipated any residual fear of death that I might have had. This was the thought of the independent Catholic philosopher Miguel de Unamuno whose soul I hope is still flourishing.

What exactly is metaphysical reality? I think it must refer to all forms of consciousness, human or otherwise. Since we may presume that *Homo sapiens* has the highest form of consciousness, he must possess the greatest degree of metaphysical reality. Whether there is a metaphysical reality outside of consciousness is an open question. If there is a God in the Judeo-Christian sense of the term, He must be the ultimate metaphysical reality. However I can't speak to this question since I have no experience or awareness of such a God. If there is a transcendental Holy Spirit, it must be pure metaphysical reality. This latter is a more intelligible conception in my view.

14

Completed rereading Unamuno's *Tragic Sense of Life*. It is probably forty years since I last read it. It has a greater impact on me now than forty years ago. Unamuno considers all the *important* questions of life in a truly existential manner. He could have omitted the chapter on "Practical Problems" since he is not the person to deal with practical problems. One senses that he would have approved of the return today of the Spanish Inquisition. But as a stimulus to philosophical thought, he has few equals.

One of his equals was Nicholas Berdyaev. It is astonishing to me that Berdyaev, who is very erudite and mentions many obscure authors, does not mention Unamuno in any of his books. Their lives were contemporaneous and many of their concerns and opinions were identical. Unamuno has been called the Spanish Dostoevsky—Berdyaev should have been interested in him. Unamuno was widely translated during Berdyaev's lifetime and probably better known than the latter. His omission in Berdyaev's discussions is a mystery to me.

* * *

An increasingly disturbing occurrence to me is that I am often sleepy during the day. It is as though I am never fully awake. Why is this? My age? Not enough sleep at night? Understimulation? Alcohol? (Like most people of Russian descent, I have a weakness for vodka.) Probably a combination of all of these factors. There is not much I can do about any of them. I don't feel I can any longer do sustained creative writing—except the brief entries in this journal. Petrarch says that at his advanced age (he was younger than I), reading and writing were the only things left that gave him pleasure. I have read virtually everything of interest to me, so writing is all that is left.

15

Both Unamuno and Berdyaev think that the principal problem of philosophy is the question of eschatology—of the *end*, of death, of immortality. Berdyaev is more concerned with eschatology of humanity as a whole, while Unamuno thinks more of his own end. But both wrestle with the problem of individual destiny.

I cannot concern myself with the fate of humanity, since the term has no emotional meaning for me. Intellectually, I know what the word means but there is no accompanying feeling. Moreover, I know there are vast differences between myself and other people. With only occasional exceptions, others seem to belong to a different species. The similarity of DNA is not significant when it comes to souls. I can only speak for myself—and perhaps a very few like-minded others.

For myself, I do not believe—I cannot believe—that my biological death will be the end of me. What an anticlimax to my spiritual life that would be if it were the case! But I do not think it is true. The soul exists within a different dimension of reality than does the body; therefore, it must have its own destiny. I feel this in the very core of my being. But time will tell. Meanwhile, I live *as if* upon death everything about me will be totted up, but it will not be finality for my soul.

I do not share the apocalyptic visions of Berdyaev or Unamuno's irrational Christian eschatology of immortality of both body and soul. My personality is a simple one; it has a limited perspective. I am only a good foot soldier in the ranks of eternity. I do not desire more than simple spiritual survival.

16

I have satisfied myself that the human self or soul—my soul—is an existent entity albeit existing in a different dimension of existence than a material one. The question of the *persistence* of the soul following death of the body is a more difficult one to engage. There are several possibilities to consider: 1) the soul is an epiphenomenon of the neurological system and disappears into the air upon death; 2) the soul transmigrates into another body, animal or human; 3) the soul enters into another abode (heaven or hell) depending on how the individual lives his life; 4) the soul rejoins the Divinity from which it arose, thereby enriching Divinity and perpetuating its own being.

I dismiss the first three possibilities as being irrational, childish, or merely imaginative. The fourth, however, merits serious consideration as it has been the conclusion of certain profound thinkers and mystics. Nevertheless, I have not yet been able to persuade myself of the *reality* of this belief. The idea is a noble one, and therefore enticing, but the nobility or enticement of an idea does not make it real. Truth is the final arbiter of all beliefs. I do not hold with the pragmatic theory of truth that says that a useful or beneficial idea is one that is true. I have concluded I will have to wait for death to find out what happens to my soul. If it disappears completely, then none of all this is relevant. But I think I will find out. "Truth will out," as Shakespeare says forcefully in one of his dramas.

17

A Biological Rumination: Life cannot be explained by physical or biological "scientific" theories. All matter and energy tend toward maximal entropy—that is, maximal homogeneity. But life tends toward heterogeneity with increasing complexity of organisms. Sophistical explanations based on chance or probability theories are implausible, to say the least. Only a metaphysical life force, an *élan vital* (Bergson) existing outside the realm of scientific demonstration can explain life.

The germplasm of humans is the substrate upon which the life force "alights" and connects to the material realm of existence. How this happens is an eternal mystery, beyond human comprehension. Life-bearing male spermatocytes enter life-bearing female ova in the female genital tract to initiate the development of a human being. In favorable circumstances, development proceeds apace from the fertilized ovum to the stage of an embryo, then fetus, then newborn human individual who enters the world to become biologically independent. The metaphysical life force continues to drive the new human being through various physical and mental growth phases. At some point, the life force achieves a degree of complexity that qualifies it to be called a *soul*.

During senescence, progressive illness, or accidents, the life force that is now the soul gradually separates from the body.

Through death, the separation becomes complete. As in the case of life, science has never been able to fully explain death. It has been described but not comprehended. Only the withdrawal of a metaphysical life force provides a rational explanation of death.

The life force driving life in a human being is antecedent to it; therefore, it is reasonable to assume that this life force (or soul) can exist posterior to his death. There is every reason to assume that the soul survives biological death unless one is a dogmatic monist. But then to what end does this process occur? Decreasing entropy requires a final cause as well as efficient ones. Metempsychosis (transmigration) or entry into special abodes for souls (heaven, hell) are ways of thought that have no basis in experience or reason. They are most unlikely possibilities.

More and more, I suspect the human life force or soul returns from whence it arose—Divinity or ultimate reality. The soul after a life experience *enriches* Divinity, thereby rewarding it for the gift of participation in human life. This may be wishful thinking but it is a reflective wishful thinking. Therefore, I think it is incumbent upon human souls to develop themselves to the greatest extent possible during their participation in biological living, given all the opportunities available to them during this period. In the terminology of pragmatism, *the idea works* as a way toward personal fulfillment.

* * *

No doubt the bold idea described above might not exactly conform to the reality, but I believe that something like it is true, something likely to be quite unexpected. It is a worthy belief to which the most intellectually scrupulous individual can adhere without apology. This thought may contradict former beliefs of mine, but it is the prerogative of a philosopher to move on with his ideas and beliefs.

Without a concept of the *meaning* of life—in Aristotelian terms, the *final cause*—a human being will be provided one by his society. It will then be based on societal values, not personal values.

18

I am still reading intensively in Lev Shestov. His conviction that the scientific method of thought is enslaving humanity is interesting; in my view, there is much truth to it, although I would not include all philosophy in his blanket condemnation of this category. His desire to substitute faith for science is very vague. He never specifies what kind of faith he means, except that it involves faith in "God." All knowledgeable individuals know where unrestrained faith in God can lead. All in all, I am not persuaded by Shestov's ideas in spite of his vast erudition—the latter overdone I think.

* * *

The feeling I treasure is that my soul exists and one day will become part of an ultimate metaphysical reality (Divinity, God). This is the only form of "grace" that has been vouchsafed to me. Instead of a passive faith in God, I must make something of my spiritual self in order to enrich Divinity waiting for it. It doesn't tell me what to think or do; I must discover these things for myself.

19

The term "grace" has been lightly thrown out to explain my conviction about the destiny of my soul. I have to confess that the term is really meaningless. To say that one's faith is based on divine grace is like the doctors' in Moliere's *The Imaginary Invalid* use of the term "sleep-inducing property" to explain why opium induces sleep. Molière ridiculed the pompous doctors of his day because they resorted to fancy Latin or Greek terms as substitutes for their lack of understanding of diseases. The term "grace" falls into this category of sophistry. It only means that the reason for one's faith is not evident to the observer. To attribute faith in God to a gift from God is not different from the practices of the medical doctors in Molière's comedy. It conceals ignorance and gives one's faith an appearance of a divine endorsement that is quite unjustified. Even worse, it demeans human spirituality along with metaphysics in general.

* * *

In my judgment, *Oberman* by the French writer Senancour (1804) is one of the greatest European literary achievements. Today it is hardly known, not to speak of being read. It is difficult to categorize it but it must be one of the first truly existential works of literature. One might compare it to Kerouac's *On The Road* but it is far more philosophically profound than Kerouac's writing—besides the deep differences in the protagonist's world-view. However, one reads *Oberman* for the same reason he reads *On The Road;* it is an entry into the mind of a strong-souled individual.

Noumena Press has done the English-reading world a service by reprinting an English translation of the book. However, they would have done better to leave out the 1910 introduction of the translator, which expresses the most intolerant elements of the positivism of that era. Fortunately, the prefaces by Saint Beuve (1833) and George Sand (1840) have been included. They serve as far better introductions to the writings of Senancour.

20

This journal deals with my interior self, my *soul,* but there is another side to me, the objective features of my life as distinct from the subjective ones. I have not mentioned these because this is a journal of subjectivity; however, the objective features clearly form part of my personality. I have a dog to which I am quite attached. My financial circumstances are comfortable as I have a pension and collect social security. I live in a wonderful unspoiled part of the world in a cabin adequate for my needs. I am close to 80 years of age and in good health. What others call isolation, I feel to be beneficial solitude.

All this has to do with the external aspects of my existence. By most standards, I am relatively fortunate. However, my interior self exists in a different dimension of reality. My thoughts, feelings, desires, volitions, and emotions fall into this different dimension. It is as though I am a split personality, split between the objectively connected and subjectively felt elements of my existence. The French word *dédoublement* is a better one to describe my situation as it carries within it explicit reference to the doubling of my self.

Of course, all human beings exhibit this doubling of their personality to some degree. With me, however, the subjective element is very pronounced, with a corresponding diminution of the objective side. The activity of my mind is central to my being. This is why writing is so important to me, as it brings order, clarity, and a degree of continuity to my mental activity. I put my writings into manuscript format because it is the easiest way to maintain them in objective form, available to me for rereading and relearning at any time. I care little for the impact they might have on others. *Attrape qui peut*, the motto of Alfred de Vigny, has always been my attitude toward readers.

I read a great deal, but only the writings that *enliven* me, as Goethe recommended. I know little of contemporary literature or philosophy as I have found the contemporary literary scene to be distasteful and unrewarding to me. The same is true of the contemporary social scene that I reluctantly enter from time to time. Friends I have very few. It is clear that I am a person quite alienated from his society; however, I don't find this thought distressing.

I realize that my external good fortune has made the life I lead possible and for that I am grateful. The same is true for the oxygen in the air that I breathe, the foodstuffs that are available to me, the stability of my societal circumstances and the health I have enjoyed so far. The first part of my life I gave over to society with questionable results for others as well as for myself, in my opinion. The last part I have given over to fulfilling my own self with better results. I look forward to the finale of my life with curiosity and, if I may say so, with anticipation of a new and perhaps better way of being.

21

Reading *Libres Méditations* of Senancour is like a miner panning for gold: much gravel and dirt is sifted out, but also flashes of the precious metal are found. Senancour's value is timeless. His mysticism is good for one's soul; he reminds us in his first meditation that our days are almost always badly filled and do not satisfy "*l'intelligence*," by which he means the soul.

Like Schain (*Souls Exist*), I have long been persuaded of the truth that the soul is a separate reality from the brain, but then comes the question of the fate of the soul when the material body dies. Epictetus says that a person is a little soul bearing a corpse but he does not say what happens when the corpse is buried or burned. The Preacher of Ecclesiastes says the corpse inevitably becomes the dust from whence it came and the spirit returns to the God who gave it (Eccl. 12:7). Elsewhere, however, he seems unsure of the latter point (Eccl. 3:21).

In this situation, one can only resort to the time-honored reliance on intuition—the intuition that there is a meaning to the creation and development of one's metaphysical soul and that it does not share the fate of the body. As a metaphysical entity, there is no dust to which it can return. I have discarded as irrational the idea that the soul is an epiphenomenon that "evaporates" on death of the body. This is the attitude of science-indoctrinated monists who cannot conceive of a dimension of reality beyond the material one. No revelation from without has come to me with the definitive answer. But the intuition within tells me that my soul will return to the ultimate metaphysical source from whence it came and *enrich* its nature. Angelus Silesius wrote that God needs me as I have need of Him. This is the purpose, I believe, of a soul's sojourn and development in the physical world.

Of course this thinking is mystical in nature. Mysticism is an essential part of the human condition. This thinking does not violate my intellectual conscience as do crude religious dogmas. As Socrates says in the *Phaedo,* these thoughts are worthy of my allegiance. Should there be no truth to them and should my intuition have played me false, I shall not have been dishonored by holding to them.

22

Senancour wrote that the one essential idea is the idea of God, an absolute and eternal being. This, of course, is a commonplace of philosophies oriented toward religious faith. However, for once I do not agree with him. The essential idea for me is the awareness of one's own *metaphysical soul.* This is not really an idea as in the case of the idea of God, but an intimate consciousness of one's own inner reality. The implications of this consciousness or lack of it are very great. Today, when the ideological climate of scientism rejects the concept of soul, an individual's ambitions and energies are directed exclusively toward the material realities. The desire to develop one's own soul has atrophied and been replaced by materialistic goals. A different world has emerged dominated by techniques, especially computerized techniques. The human world is moving toward soullessness. One should not be deceived by false claims of spiritual values when no one truly believes in the existence of spirit. Dogmatic religions with traditional moralities may still exist but they are not backed up by a genuine awareness of the existence of a personal soul. One can *believe* in God but one has to be *aware* of his soul. Otherwise, materialism inevitably will reign supreme.

23

I use the term "soul" so often that I need to develop a clearer picture of just what I mean by it. To me, it is essentially equivalent to mind or self, but I prefer to say soul because the word has traditional connotations that should not be abandoned. It conjures up feelings of holiness, sanctity, and meaning. True, it is associated with Christian dogmas of dubious value, but this does not mean the term should be abandoned. It clothes the interior self of a human being with dignity.

The principal characteristic of the soul is consciousness. Consciousness can exist on many levels. There is the consciousness that is opposed to unconsciousness; one is either in one or the other state, where the distinction is quite evident. Another type of consciousness is that induced by sensory stimuli: visual, auditory, tactile, etc., which have clear causative antecedents. The antecedents of internal visceral stimuli are not so clear but they too contribute to consciousness. Sensory stimuli produce images in the conscious mind of the person stimulated. Ever since Kant, it has become clear that these images may not correlate at all with the unknown causative realities (*noumena* in Kantian terminology). This realization should produce humility in observers with respect to their knowledge of the external world.

The events involved in the production of visual images have been worked out in great detail by neurophysiologists. The visual stimuli from objects are carried by light waves to the optic retina of the seeing subject, where they cause firing of the optic nerve attached to the retina. These are carried by optic nerve tracts to the visual cortex in the rear of the brain. At that point, something happens to translate the neural activity into a visual image in the mind. How this occurs is as mysterious as the beginning of the universe or the origins of life. It is a form of "transfiguration" in which physical events are transformed into metaphysical images. This "miracle" is a constant occurrence in all living creatures that see. Similar scenarios can be constructed for the other kinds of sensory stimuli.

Besides images, there are other, more complex aspects of the content of consciousness in sentient humans. Instincts, ideas, values, and thoughts of all kinds may fill their souls. Affective content refers to emotions, desires, and volitions. Schopenhauer believed that the soul was fundamentally "will," but he later expanded his view to include compassion. There have been many descriptions and definitions of the human soul. However, there is no simple formula that does full justice to its nature.

Finally, one must distinguish between objective neurophysiology and psychology on the one hand, and the immediate consciousness of one's own soul or self-consciousness on the other. In the latter, the subjective consciousness and the object of its attention are one and the same. How this can be is another mystery pertaining to the activity of the human soul. But without self-consciousness and without accompanying reverence for one's own soul, the individual becomes just another pawn in the ongoing comedy of the world around him.

24

I recently read Paul Claudel's very moving account of his conversion to Catholicism. It occurred suddenly when he was in the Cathedral of Notre Dame in Paris. His personality had been prepared beforehand and was suited to this event. I think all individuals should come in their own way to a consciousness of the ultimate realities. Mine is quite different from that of Christianity, or for that matter, Judaism. For me, Divinity—I have come to prefer that term to God—is my belief expressing the unifying metaphysical force acting within the universe. I prefer to form my own idea of this force rather than accepting the ones of traditional religions. My individuality in this crucial area is paramount. Furthermore, I believe that my individual soul is *needed* by Divinity, just as my soul needs it in order to exist. All the talk of grace, revelation, prayer, and faith are just so many obstacles to my personal idea about Divinity. Without this idea, I am left to the mercies of the societal culture.

"Culture" is a metaphysical concept like Divinity, but it is far more involved with the material world than is Divinity, which is a purely metaphysical concept. Culture is involvement with *hoi polloi*, culture is the province of religion and the literary guilds, culture is bought by wealth and utilized by power. For me, my own concept of Divinity is more important than the accoutrements of culture, whether religious or secular. Berdyaev asserted that "Culture" was a great failure; he thought that religious creativity was the only salvation for civilization. I would hope that he might have seen my ideas as a form of religious creativity.

Schopenhauer coined the famous phrase, "Religion is the metaphysics of the people." I have no wish to intrude on anyone's metaphysics. But I would like to obtain respect for my own metaphysics, including the way of life that is part of it.

Religious dogmatists often fulminate against "relativism" in religion. "What is truth?" is a question that has preoccupied philosophers and bothered theologians in all times. It was the question, put perhaps sarcastically, that Pontius Pilate, a cultured Roman administrator, put to Jesus—who seemed not to have answered. An answer would have served no purpose in the situation. Pragmatic philosophers say truth is what works in the world. Contemporary physics casts doubt on all the naïve truths accepted in the past about the nature of the physical universe. In my opinion, Pilate had the right attitude. Absolute truth cannot be ascertained by human beings. One can only state one's own beliefs and values, which are determined by one's inner self, one's soul. This is why the development of the soul is important for every individual. This is the heart of my metaphysical existentialism.

25

A little Bible discussion. I am convinced that consciousness of one's relationship to Divinity is the key to a fulfilling life. No matter how skeptical, every human soul seeks ultimately to become conscious of this relationship. The *Sh'ma* of Judaism with its great commandments is the biblical expression of this insight. "Hear O Israel, the Lord is our God, the Lord alone," followed by, "Love the Lord thy God with all thy heart and all thy soul and all thy strength" (Deut. 6:4-5). Jesus saw fit to quote from it when asked by a scribe, which was the first of all commandments (Mark 12:28-30). The *Sh'ma* is the most important of all Jewish prayers and is the foundation of Judeo-Christian religions. Even Spinoza who had rejected both religions asserted that the "intellectual love of God" was the highest manifestation of the human spirit.

The difficulty with the traditional concept of Divinity, the one that most often is the underlying reason for atheism, is the notion of blind subservience of an individual to an almighty Deity. It is not hard science but psychology that cannot abide the idea of a God who is absolute ruler of the universe and all within it. Few intelligent scientists resist the concept of an ultimate reality or prime mover or first cause that can be named "God." But the thought of human individuals as permanent children needing guidance and forgiveness from a "compassionate" deity is repugnant to independent spirits. A spiritually mature individual does not want a savior. Nor can he be a "slave of Christ" or anyone else. Not prayer, not sacrifices, not rituals or liturgies, not even love is what he wishes to offer to Divinity. What he has to offer is more precious than all of the above; he has his *soul* to offer. Divinity needs human souls for its fulfillment. The mystic Angelus Silesius poeticized that Divinity *cannot exist* without human souls (*Der Cherubinischer Wandermann).*

The place of Divinity in society, however it is named, is a recurrent theme in the history of civilizations. The development of culture, especially scientific culture, is often seen as a replacement for religion, but cultures have all been a failure in this regard. Culture that does not lead to consciousness of Divinity sooner or later becomes mere entertainment and brings out the worst in the human spirit. Greek and Roman cultures became failures, the Renaissance became a failure, the great European culture of recent centuries has led to two disastrous World Wars and constant strife in the world. And organized religions, which were supposed to advance the human condition to a higher plane of existence, have all been failures. It is time for development of a "religion"—the term distresses me but I can find no other—that puts the metaphysical human soul on a similar footing with Divinity; that gives divine status to the developed soul. (*Honi soit qui mal y pense.*)

The only purpose to the human enterprise, as I see it, is to form new souls. This is so because its originator, Divinity, needs souls. It needs the infusion of new spiritual blood formed out of the struggles of human existence. I can think of no other reasonable explanation for the phenomenon of man. The details of this insight are beyond my ken, but that is no objection to its basic validity. The oft-quoted vision of Psalm 19 asserts: "The heavens declare the glory of God, the skies proclaim the work of his hands." The Psalmist might have added that beyond the heavens and skies, it is human souls that form the real basis for this glory.

26

I take understanding the formation of my soul most seriously and have given considerable thought to this question. It has seemed to me that the path to take for this knowledge is to determine the main activities to which I have consciously or unconsciously devoted myself during the course of my life. In the matter of formation of my soul, I trust my instincts to have done what is necessary and what continues to be necessary. Three major areas can be identified:

Surprisingly, erotic experience. The desire to merge in one way or another with a woman has been with me as long as I can remember (*Verschmelzungs-Sehnsucht* is the full-throated expression of erotic longing by the philosopher

E. von Hartmann)—and is with me still. I remember thinking when I read Schain's essay "The Meaning of the Erotic Impulse" (*Philosophical Artwork*, 1983) that it was completely valid for me. Briefly, I feel that one strives to overcome gender incompleteness by merging with the opposite sex. (The phenomenon of homosexuality is a mystery to me.) Eroticism, I believe, is a *metaphysical* phenomenon expressed through a variety of physical and psychological means of which coupling with the object of desire is only one form. Through erotic experiences, the soul is refreshed, expanded, and tends toward completion. The fact that societal influences can demean these experiences does not detract from their fundamental meaning. These thoughts were expressed by Plato in mythic form in his *Symposium*, but they have never been a myth for me; they have been a constant reality throughout much of my life. Were it not for eroticism, my life might have been characterized by a much greater solitude.

Reading. Books have for me been the main avenue leading to the vast world of thought. Through reading, I have gained access to the soul of many great-souled individuals. I have read voraciously: novels, poetry, biography, autobiography, philosophy, theology. I have devoted a great deal of energy to learning to read foreign languages in order not to be dependent upon translations. It is one of the sorrows of my life that I have not succeeded in learning to read Russian as I feel this language contains much of the truly profound literature of the world. But I have not yet abandoned this effort.

I cannot imagine what my life would have been without books. It would have been like being raised in a small room without windows. I have learned to read only books that *enliven* me, meaning to expand my soul, as Goethe advised. These can be any form of writing but more and more are confined to existential philosophy. Recently, the writings of Nicholas Berdyaev have been an important formative influence on my mind. But there have been others that are too numerous to mention.

Writing. My devotion to writing stems from my experience that writing strengthens, enlarges, and solidifies my soul. I am constantly learning about myself through my writings. Furthermore, one of the most important means by which I learn is through rereading my former writings. When one genuinely expresses oneself in writing, he is transforming many formless aspects of his soul into recognizable features. This is a great benefit to self-consciousness, the most important quality of the soul. (In common usage, the term "self-conscious" expresses a negative judgment!) It is also through writing that I have come to realize the existence of an ultimate Divinity, a term whose meaning for me I have previously described in this journal. I like to imagine that I have more to offer Divinity through writing, since this activity gives form to what had previously been vague and uncertain.

27

The close relationship of my soul to Divinity is fundamental to my view of the world. This feeling stems from the depths of my soul; it is not based on any scientifically-validated "facts," nor on any "revelations," nor on any "grace" granted from above. If I do not accept this intuition, what can I accept about anything? Lev Shestov built his philosophical reputation on combating the dominance of logical rationality over the human soul (*Athens and Jerusalem*, 1932). He turned to the Bible for inspiration, but this is not the case with me. My inspiration comes from within. It is impossible for me to form a conception of my soul without a conception of its groundwork that I call Divinity. If the soul is not an evanescent breath of air deriving from the activity of my cerebral neurons, it must be related to a larger metaphysical reality. The question is: "What is this reality and what is the nature of this relationship?'

The Abrahamic religions—Judaism, Christianity, Islam—have based their faiths on man's dependence upon God. The ultimate goal in life according to them is carrying out his will, a servile concept of faith if there ever was one. But God is said to have created man in his image, which is not that of a slave. As Berdyaev has written, "God is the liberator [of man]; Theology has made a slave of him" (*Slavery and Freedom*, 1937). In the model of Christianity, God has created an overseer, Jesus Christ, who supervises this slavery. I do not think this metaphor is excessive.

The relationship of Divinity to the human soul should be as equals, to utilize another metaphor, as a mature son is to his father. There is no place here for subservience. The relationship is between equals rather than monarch to subjects. Hindu Vedanta was far more insightful when it coined the aphorism "Atman is Brahman," meaning God and the individual soul ultimately are one.

My position is based upon an overriding intuition that I am an independent entity, that I possess free will, and that my value does not lie in being a subservient creature of Divinity. God is not my tyrannical father; he is a traditional elder to be respected but not obeyed. He is more like Zeus than Jehovah. The spark of Divinity with which I began independent life is a derivative of the metaphysical energy from below, the *Ungrund* postulated by Jacob Boehme, which is represented in the universe by Divinity. The mystical "I" feels this similarity in its depths. It is microcosmic life yearning toward macrocosmic existence.

This avowedly mystical consciousness affects my entire physical and mental life. I am proud of the appellation of *mystic* since I think it is a form of consciousness superior to logical thought, which is becoming more and more irrelevant to the human condition. I do not fear death since this will only be a release from an aging body to a transfigured form of existence. I am not subject to the tyrannies of religion or culture since I do not depend on these to give meaning to my life. I strive to create my own soul. I aim toward that goal fervently sought after by *Homo sapiens*: to be a spiritual person.

28

Vasily Grossman's novel *Life and Fate* depicts the situation in Russia during World War II. It may be the greatest Russian historical novel since Tolstoy's *War and Peace*, which it resembles in many ways. His description of the German extermination apparatus is heart-rending. Grossman's discussion of death, however, reveals him as a writer to be a product of Socialist Realism.

Grossman believes in the epiphenomenon theory of consciousness, although for him it was probably not a theory, but a self-evident fact. He has no awareness or interest in a metaphysical dimension of the human condition; no doubt he dismissed the concept as religious superstition. He was a prisoner of the materialist worldview. "When a person dies, he crosses over from the realm of freedom to the realm of slavery…consciousness first weakens and then disappears…the universe inside a person has ceased to exist." But Grossman does not really know what happens to the human soul upon death and his mind is not able to envision a metaphysical reality. In this respect, he is akin to a vast number of people under the spell of scientism.

If a person can only envision reality through the senses and thinks there can be no other reality, then his attitude toward death will be similar to Grossman's. But there is no rational reason why a soul must invariably share the fate of the body and when the latter ceases to exist, it ceases to exist. When the stalk from which an ear of corn has arisen is cut and dies, the ear of corn still exists and will proceed to its destiny as food or seeding new cornstalks—or perhaps disintegrate in time. The ear of corn is a material object so there is no difficulty in perceiving its ultimate fate. The soul, however, is not a material object; it is a metaphysical entity, uniquely a product of the human condition. It cannot be perceived with the senses. Upon death of the body, it must enter into a new dimension of reality—one that seems impossible for living human beings to perceive or even imagine. Perhaps it must separate from the body for it to fully flourish.

Jesus is quoted in scripture as having said, "unless a kernel of corn falls to the ground, it remains alone; but if it 'dies', it then bears much fruit" (John 12:24). Everyone must decide for himself the relevance of this metaphor to the problem of the fate of the soul upon death of the body.

29

Desire and discipline are the two prime forces in my life. One or the other is dominant at various times but if either should completely disappear, I fear my life would become a shambles.

* * *

It is my humble opinion as an ethnic Jew that Moses, the great prophet of Judaism, led the Jews down a wrong path that eventually marginalized them in the world. Although the details of his personality are shrouded in the haze of remote antiquity, it seems that Moses established the precedent of imposing on the Hebrew people the rituals, ceremonies, legalisms, and especially separateness that eventually grew to dominate their religion. It has remained so to this day in religious Jewry. Spiritual development is impeded under such circumstances. It was against this situation that Jesus rebelled and preached the primacy of spirituality.

It is ironic that the followers of Jesus, starting with Peter and Paul, recapitulated the development of Judaic legalism—later substituting a replaceable Pope for Moses and adding the mythic figure of Christ Jesus, "Son of God," as the indispensable savior of the individual. To Jewry, however, this last feature was seen as idolatry and blasphemy, and caused them to reject forever an individual who had started out as a prophet in the tradition of the great Jewish prophets of yesteryear. Thus Judaism lost its greatest religious figure, bar none.

All this reveals the danger of listening to those who claim special divine revelation. Divinity never tells people what they should or should not believe or do. Belief and action are solely the responsibility of one's own self.

30

For more than a century now, high-energy microphysics has been revealing how far removed from reality are our common-sense perceptions of the world around us. What we perceive as stable material objects are really whirling masses of micro-phenomena: electrons, neutrons, positrons, and who knows what else. The instruments of microphysics seem endlessly capable of discovering tinier and tinier corpuscular entities. Even the traditional concept of matter has been brought into question; quantum field theory has asserted that "matter" may really be composed of unstable packets of energy rather than defined particles. The distinction between matter and non-matter, between matter and energy and, by extension, between matter and spirit becomes quite vague. Mathematics seems to be a better tool for understanding these instrument-based concepts than are our crude unaided sensory perceptions.

It is no different with our commonsense perception of space and time. Einstein's general relativity theory has shown that all the unaided perceptions of positions of objects in space and time are relative to our own positions; there are no absolute realities as far as human beings are concerned. Not only that, but the old theory of a four-dimensional universe has given way to an awareness that there are numerous dimensions in which physical reality may exist.

Given this explosion of new insights into the nature of reality, it is evident that commonsense ideas about the soul are not to be relied upon. Metaphysics as a form of reality is surely no less complex than physics. The idea that the internal psychic reality traditionally called the soul is merely an epiphenomenon of the physical brain is only a consequence of the "commonsense" idea that what cannot be perceived by the senses does not exist. This is quite a simplistic idea, hardly deserving of discussion. Commonsense thinking may be a benefit in daily living, but it is a positive hindrance in understanding the nature of the universe. Equally, such imaginative ideas that upon death the soul flies to a heavenly paradise or descends to a fearful hell must be thrown out of court. These dogmas are unworthy of modern thought. The reality is that the details of the fate of the soul in the cosmic scheme of things are quite unknown. One's imagination can be brought into play, but dogmatic or commonsense conclusions are worthless.

31

Sometimes I feel that I have little more to gain from reading. Whatever there may be of value in literature or philosophy, I have already assimilated. There is certainly nothing for me in the playgrounds of contemporary fiction. Further reading for me is like muscle building beyond any useful purpose and only kills time that could be put to better use. At my age, I cannot afford to kill time.

Writing is now the most reliable route for developing myself. It is a form of self-exploration leading to my own metaphysical development. When I express myself in writing, new forms of consciousness emerge like unfamiliar creatures from the deep. I believe that the *meaning* of development of the metaphysical self has not yet been ascertained in Western culture. This is not surprising, especially today when the cult of scientism has destroyed awareness of the reality of the soul. Like Oberman, there is nothing left for me but to write. "Write what?" one may ask. Write what is fermenting within me, I answer.

Periodically, it is necessary for me to take stock of my life. I have to avoid losing myself in the mire of details involved in the technological existence today. Henry David Thoreau preached simplicity, simplicity, and more simplicity, and I try to follow his recommendation. That is not easy to do in the contemporary world, even under my relatively simple present circumstances.

Since I am retired from the work-for-pay lifestyle and have the inestimable advantage of a secure income, I must also recognize the dangers inherent in such a life. I am no longer exposed to most of the stresses of American societal life—stresses that have a certain benefit for strengthening one's soul. "Life is strife," according to Empedocles, and without strife, one can fall into a sloth-like state for which the only remedy is death. I feel, however, that a heightened consciousness of the human condition, and thus one's own condition, brings its own stress in the form of dissatisfaction with one's condition, and the uncertainty of not knowing how to improve it. The urge to expand one's own soul and make it worthy of the ultimate goal of human life—whatever that may be—brings with it a type of stress unknown to a mediocre way of life. My own life has revealed this to be true.

32

The guiding light of my life is development of my soul. I have defined earlier in this journal what I mean by "soul." All societal obligations, responsibilities, and inducements are secondary to this overriding purpose. Some will see this as the credo of a savage individualism but, in the marrow of my being, I believe my soul must come first. Secondary responsibilities require attention but, for me, they are always secondary. This is a credo I have come by gradually in the course of my life. Even if I do not know what will ultimately come of my soul, my instinct to develop it at whatever cost cannot be ignored.

The nineteenth century Romantics of Europe suffered with *ennui* because they did not know how to deal with this instinct. Everything about the society they lived in repelled or bored them; yet they did not have an adequate conception of spiritual development to cope with it. Because of their ennui, they contemplated suicide either directly or through their fictional characters. They could not free themselves from the feeling that their lives were being wasted. Thoreau with his Yankee brevity asserted that most men lived lives of quiet desperation; Senancour had his fictional character Oberman say the same, except with the usual Gallic verbosity.

Today, "ennui" is a dated concept. Bourgeois society has hardened men's souls to a point where they are no longer capable of feeling ennui. A certain consciousness of the importance of one's soul is required for this state of mind to appear. Games, gambling, bourgeois living, and electronic screens have deadened minds so as to no longer experience ennui. Some may think this is a good thing, but I believe it is a sign of the arrested infantile state of people's souls.

There are two articles of faith to which I hold: 1) One's soul exists as a metaphysical reality deserving of the highest reverence. 2) One is required to do whatever is in one's power to deepen its substance, enlarge its dimensions, and prepare for whatever may befall it in the future.

33

Religious feelings. Once again, I realize how the Judeo-Christian-Islamic religions have retarded the metaphysical development of those who subscribe to them. Schopenhauer's well-known judgment that religion is the metaphysics of the people reveals his awareness of this unfortunate fact although he seems to have preferred not to state it directly. The individuals who have not subjected themselves to religious dogmas usually reject metaphysics entirely and turn to scientism. However, the cosmic scheme of the universe requires a *metaphysical consciousness* for an individual to flourish. One's soul develops through this consciousness. Divinity wants and needs participation by human souls. Western religions have subverted this process by postulating an almighty, all-knowing, all-controlling Deity to whom individuals are utterly subservient. These religions claim to know the "will of God," but such claims have no foundation in reality.

Christianity has added the further fiction of a "Son of God" who is the only possible savior of men's souls. This has been an additional impediment to metaphysical development of individuals, since the only possible savior of a soul is the individual himself. Eastern religions have not been burdened with these anthropomorphic ideas about Deity and teachers like Vivekananda, Sri Aurobindo, and Arvind Sharma have had far more to offer westerners in the area of religion than have Jewish rabbis or Christian pastors. I will refrain from commenting on the role of Muslim clergy in this regard.

Religious institutions, no matter how superannuated they may be, tend to follow Spinoza's rule of persistence of being. They too persist in being unless some force of great magnitude eradicates them.

The entire American society is permeated with noxious religious influences on metaphysical (spiritual) development. However, there are dangers in directly voicing this opinion. There is no longer fear of torture or death at the stake but instead there is the likelihood of alienation from society. Even if one does not subscribe to a particular religion, it is required that religious beliefs be *respected* in public expression, no matter how unworthy they are of such respect. The classic example of a public figure who attacked the Christian religion is that of Friedrich Nietzsche. His *Der Antichrist* (correct English translation is AntiChristian, not The Antichrist) has been regarded as the product of a demented individual instead of a man indignant about the harmful effects of Christianity. *Antichrist* was published after his nervous breakdown, but long before Nietzsche was criticizing Jewish and Christian religions in his writings. It is likely that Nietzsche's mental collapse was in part due to his alienation from conventional German society. One risks a great deal in publically attacking established religions.

34

How profoundly isolated I am from society! I no longer participate in the working world, which is ordinarily an important connection for individuals. My marriages ended so long ago that I can hardly remember them. Friends have either died or lost contact with me. I don't belong to any organizations or institutions. My home is in a remote part of the country and I have no neighbors. Amigo, my mongrel dog, is my sole companion. Really, my only connection with the outside world is my weekly visit to the post office and small market where I buy my provisions. My main reason for maintaining a postal box is to receive the books I order through the Internet. Ordering anything through the local library computer is a problem for me since I have never been adept at using it. So far, however, I have been able to get by.

I read much and keep a journal. Lately, I have been feeling that reading has become counterproductive for me and I am trying to cut back on the habit. In its place, I am enlarging the scope and substance of my journal.

The big question is whether contact with nature, friendship with a dog, and expressing one's thoughts in writing are sufficient for one's sanity. I have recognized the dangers of my alienation and isolation from society. The fact that one does not wish to participate in an insane world does not necessarily mean that one does not need to do so in order to preserve sanity. I don't want to go mad like Nietzsche and end up in an asylum. I couldn't stand needing caretakers and being stared at like an animal in a zoo.

35

My fanaticism about my soul has led me to choose isolation in order to protect it from the ravages of a status-hungry, possession-obsessed society. "Relationships" is the byword of the intelligentsia of today—family relationships, career relationships, social relationships, etc., but I have found that the relationships I have had generally have done me no good. When Emerson advised Henry David Thoreau that it would be good for the latter's health to move out more into society, the latter responded that the society he had already had made him ill. This was referring to the milieu of the transcendentalists of early 19th century New England, a group that has never been surpassed in intellectual and spiritual interests. What would Thoreau have said today!

I have staked my soul on choosing to be separate from my society. When I was younger, I chose otherwise, which perhaps was then necessary. If my society were to be a different one, I might choose differently now. But fate has placed me within one of the unremittingly materialist societies of the world. I feel that to preserve my soul, I must protect myself from it. If I did not believe in the reality of my soul, which is generally the case of those around me, and if I did not believe that it was worth protecting, I would take the path of least resistance and tread the path of the crowds. But I believe my soul has a cosmic significance, is vulnerable to materialism, and needs to be shielded from its noxious influences. Just as a virtuous maiden feels she must protect her virginity for an important liaison in her life, so I feel I must protect my soul for an important purpose—even if I am not clear on the nature of this purpose.

No doubt my point of view may seem to many to be narcissistic at best and verging on madness. Perhaps I am mad. But I have made my wager even if it is not the one Pascal advised and I will accept the consequences. As was said by a famous Christian rebel who was slightly mad himself, "*Hier stehe ich, Ich kann nicht anders*" ("Here I stand. I can do no other").

36

There are two overriding issues that every spiritually-minded person must face—the existence and nature of God and the existence and nature of the soul. Both of these questions must be confronted by individuals serious about their own existence. These are metaphysical issues that cannot be solved by contemporary scientism.

It is unfortunate that thought on these questions has been suppressed by religious institutions. The Judaic approach was established earlier on in Judaism when all believers in competing Gods were exterminated to the best of the ability of the Hebrew tribes. When Christianity (a Jewish sect) became the official religion of the Roman Empire, again all competing metaphysical thought was forcefully suppressed. Roman Catholic Christianity was the only permissible metaphysical ideology and remained so in Europe for over a thousand years.

The emergence of the Renaissance and Humanism, first in Italy and then in other European nations, seemed to herald the resumption of free philosophical thought that had characterized the "pagan" culture of the Greek world and the pre-Christian Roman Empire. However, once again, the Christian Protestant Reformation and the Catholic Counterreformation put an end to independent metaphysical thinking, in both oral and published expression. It took burning at the stake only a few heretics and philosophers to end the Renaissance in philosophy. Thomas Aquinas was apotheosized as the "official" philosopher of Catholicism. The Protestant world limited theology to what could be found in the Bible. Jakob Burckhardt in his monumental work *Civilization of the Renaissance in Italy* showed how the Roman Inquisition and the Spanish fanatical overlords cowed independent thinking in Renaissance Italy. The Christian Churches—Catholic, Protestant and Orthodox—believed they had a monopoly on metaphysical religious thought through Christian traditions. They disputed among themselves but mainly they prevented the emergence of a non-Christian metaphysics.

This situation is little changed today. There may be no more incineration of heretics, but the climate of unacceptability of independent metaphysics has not been altered among the masses of peoples, especially in America. Scientism is the only refuge for those who reject traditional religions. A *modus vivendi* has been reached in the Western world between scientism and established religions.

37

At the end of the remarkable Hebrew scripture called Ecclesiastes, there is a little epilogue, doubtless added later by some devout Jew in order to weaken the writing's basic impact. It says: "Of making many books, there is no end and much study wearies the flesh." I do not think the writer of Ecclesiastes, whoever he may have been, would have agreed to this addendum disparaging what he had to say. He must have felt the compulsion to express himself, as do all serious writers, and he would not have cared about rabbis or scholars engaged in wearying their flesh. In the best of all worlds, every individual will have something special to express and should do so publicly to the best of one's abilities.

The addendum adds, "Fear God and keep his commandments, for this is the whole duty of man." Here lies the source of all the problems produced by the Abrahamic religions. No one should ever fear God since he does not punish us and we cannot keep his commandments, because there are none. God does not command or punish. These anthropomorphisms have no place in a truly spiritual concept of God. Should by some special miracle "God's commandments" were to appear, a most unlikely event, religious institutions are the last place I would expect to find them.

* * *

I have never experienced any direct contact with Deity, so my approach to Him (or Her) must be purely intellectual. This is probably the best approach since any revelation, grace, or the like produces grave doubts as to the reliability of the recipient. It seems to me, however, that there must be a larger metaphysical reality than that of my own soul or any other individual soul. It is absurd to imagine that the entire universe is material in nature and yet we humans possess unique metaphysical souls. There must be a greater metaphysical dimension to existence that is not available to human senses. This greater dimension can be called "Divinity." Beyond that, I am unable to go.

The dogmas of Christianity—God the Father, Jesus Christ his only begotten son, his virgin Mother, the panoply of saints, the Bible as literal words of God, the Pope as his infallible interpreter—all this is just myth-making to me—and not very high quality myth. But I am willing to subscribe to my kinsman Spinoza's *amor Dei intellectualis,* as long as the deity does not tyrannize over me.

Regarding the concept requiring a "monistic" universe, there is no reason to demand that an underlying reality, an *Urgrund*, be purely material in nature. It may be composed of material, metaphysical, and perhaps many other dimensions. Because I cannot with common-sense thinking visualize such a reality, it is easier for me for practical purposes to take a dualistic approach and separate the phenomena of existence that I know about into material and spiritual elements. This may well be an oversimplification based on my limited perspective. But it is the best I can do.

The possibilities for philosophical creativity of a great mind freed from dogmatic Judeo-Christian domination is illustrated in the writings of Benedict (Baruch) Spinoza. He was equally reviled by the Jewish and Christian religious establishments. He was defamed as an atheist in spite of the quotation from him given above. For Spinoza, the so-called "will of God" was only a sanctuary of ignorance and despotism. His life, short as it was, and his work serve as an inspiration for all those individuals who wish to live their lives independently and think freely about the larger issues of life.

38

Seated at my desk at night in my cabin, surrounded only by the hooting of owls and yip-yipping of coyotes, I meditate on the nature of my existence and the nature of the society on whose fringes I live. Whenever I am tempted to leave my isolated life and return to societal activities, the sign over the portals of Hell in Dante's *Inferno* comes to my mind: *"Lasciate ogni speranza, voi ch'entrate"*—Abandon all hope, ye that enter. Then I realize the good that I have here in my remote, isolated existence. I am free to realize myself and grasp the connection of my own soul to an ultimate reality. I can envision the true nature of the world and comprehend my relationship to it. These are the real issues of human life. Today, they have been drowned out by the noises of technological society and its contempt for metaphysical questions. I have had my experiences, have had my share of achievements and failures in societal life. It was long overdue for me to leave behind that society in which I was reared in order to obtain a better place in the universe. I have entered upon the life for which I was created, the *actively contemplated* life. Now I can be at peace with myself.

Without my journal, I might never have known who and what I am.

* * *

If by chance, someone else should read the thoughts entered here, they might think of me as a person following the Hindu tradition of leaving a householder existence in order to enter the life of a hermit meditating in the forest. Doubtless, there are similarities but I consider myself to be American to the core. Walt Whitman, R.W. Emerson, H. D. Thoreau, Robinson Jeffers, Alan Watts, and Gary Snyder all showed affinities with Hindu thought but they were all Americans to their core. I know about these individuals because they have become cultural icons but there must have been many other Americans who were the same. All human beings belong to the species *Homo sapiens* so naturally there are similarities in individuals' reactions to their societies. We all tread the same earth and live under the same sky. I know I have developed myself according to my own rhythms of life and only later learned of my affinities to other individuals.

The fact that America has not perceived my existence is of no consequence. I am still a part of it. It may be that there is some vast scheme in which I play a role, although what that role might be is a mystery to me.

39

There is one person who regularly visits me in my forest retreat. Gustavo is a middle-aged Mexican who lives in a small village on the other side of the border. Periodically, he carries a backpack filled with bags of marijuana to a truck that brings them to a receiver in Tucson. The delivery is always at night to a prearranged place where Gustavo exchanges his load for dollars. I don't know more details than these and don't want to know any more. Gustavo is what is called a "mule" although he is far from mule-like. He seems to have worked out an agreement with the area "Cartel" to make modest deliveries of its product. Gustavo is getting older and does not like the risks so he keeps his deliveries small-scale, just enough to help his unemployed son and his single-mother daughter put rice and beans on their tables—plus *cerveza* on his.

I met Gustavo early in his career as a mule when he had gotten lost in the wilds of the Coronado wilderness. It was unusually hot and he had run out of water. He knocked at my door asking for a drink. The few people who live in this area don't like to help illegal crossers because the belief is prevalent that if you help one, others will follow. I haven't found this to be true as is the case with most of the fears about *illegales*. Anyway, Gustavo seemed to be decent-looking and so utterly exhausted that I allowed him in and gave him water and a place to rest. I haven't spread this around because I don't want visits from the Border Patrol who cover this area.

Every few weeks, Gustavo stops by when he needs a rest or a drink. In the beginning, he wanted to give me money, but of course I wouldn't take it. That's all I would need is to be discovered as a paid part of a drug smuggling activity! The terrain is quite hilly here and it is hard for someone Gustavo's age to cover ground with a heavy backpack. But he feels he has no choice; not only does he need the money but the Cartel has let him know they would not look favorably upon his ending deliveries. "Not looking favorably" might mean a bullet in the back of the head—or worse for his family.

We sometimes talk when he visits. Gustavo lived for some years in Tucson so he speaks English adequately. I have found it interesting to see how his mind works. He is entirely focused on the here and now of his life. He wishes his son could find work nearby; he hopes the father of his grandchild would reappear and assume his responsibilities. His daughter's health is not good. He has an old motorcycle that breaks down frequently. His roof leaks during the summer monsoon rains. There are some good things in Gustavo's life. He is raising two pigs for market and the price of pork is rising. His little *milpa* produces a good corn crop. And so on and so forth. He rarely mentions the wife that I know he has. Once I asked about her and he said she was fine. *Muy bien.* Nothing further.

Gustavo has no interest in the national affairs of Mexico, never mind the international scene. Abstract topics like education, religion, war, and personal development were beyond him. He could read but never read any book as far as I could tell. His reading was limited to labels and signposts. He did tell me once that he had a niche for the Virgin of Guadalupe in the front of his house. When he spoke of it, his eyes and face lit up in a manner quite unusual for him. But he seemed to have no contact with priests or interest in churches.

For me, Gustavo is like a creature from another planet. There is nothing about him that I can relate to in a meaningful manner. I have a certain affection for him much like I have for my dog Amigo. If he has any depth of thought, I have yet to connect to it. But in another sense, Gustavo is *Everyman*, no different from all the other millions of ordinary people struggling to make their way in the dense forests surrounding human existence. Here is another piece of evidence that I am alienated from the human race.

40

I am constantly being torn between two tendencies in my life—the tendency toward individuality and the tendency toward universality. Universality means the effort to unite with the ultimate reality of the universe. Indian metaphysics (Brahmanism and Buddhism), Christian salvationism, Judaic elitism, and Muslim fundamentalism all could serve to make me part of a greater reality that makes little or no demands upon my individuality. On the other hand, individuality requires me to draw upon my own spiritual and intellectual resources for fulfillment. The desire for worldly success is at heart a function of individuality, since without "success," it is hard for a person to consistently maintain his individualism. By and large, the world I used to live in was committed to individuality, but it was an individuality repellant to me, an individuality that was purely materialist in nature.

Since I have achieved no worldly success, sometimes it is difficult for me to maintain an allegiance to my own way of being an individual. The temptation to immerse myself in some kind of suprapersonal faith is always there. However, the sense of my own individuality, the feeling of my own *persona,* is hard for me to give up for the sake of a comfortable universalism. I don't want to give up the awareness that I am a distinctive individual in my own right. Can my life have any meaning if I am only destined to sink into some greater whole? Lucifer in Milton's *Paradise Lost* has always attracted me more than all the cohorts of the Lord—and truth to tell, even the Lord himself.

* * *

By some chance, Jacques Maritain's *Introduction to Philosophy* has fallen into my hands. I have been trying to read it sympathetically since he is an important figure in contemporary Roman Catholic philosophy. But what arrogance! He dismisses Eastern philosophies as without "morality." This from a member of a religion that has committed immoral acts throughout most of its history. He is equally dismissive of the Pre-Socratic philosophers, of Plato, and the Stoics. He doesn't even mention twentieth century Existentialism. He presents a warmed-over, lifeless Scholasticism based on Aristotle and Aquinas as the only "true" philosophy.

Maritain says he writes principally for Christian readers for whom I feel sorry if this is the kind of pap they think philosophy to be. Myself, I turn with relief back to Emerson, Nietzsche, or Berdyaev, all of whom are worthy representatives of the great traditions of philosophic thought.

41

Once in a great while, I receive an invitation to a social event—a party, a reception, or even a dinner at the home of a writer with whom I have had some contact on occasion. We both have Russian origins so we have that in common. He lives a few miles away; I don't know how he became aware of my solitary existence and my philosophical interests, but he has and must feel a charitable impulse toward me. I usually accept out of some perverse motive since I know that I will never find the event either pleasant or stimulating. The most I can hope for is free liquor and, sometimes, a good meal.

The types at these events are what can be loosely classified as "intellectuals"—university faculty, authors, doctors, lawyers—the latter two groups as intellectuals only by a mighty stretch of one's imagination. I put on my one set of good clothes and social mask and try to be sociable. This would be impossible without a heavy dose of spirits during the event. The people there always strike me in the same way—smug, self-righteous, opinionated, ignorant "intelligentsia" who are disinterested in or unaware of the real nature of the human condition or even their own condition. No doubt some of them might be different in private but put them in a social setting and they are intolerable. Of course, they wouldn't be interested in a sustained private contact with a person like me who is a dropout from society. All of them really just want to network with influential people. Every time I return home from one of these events I vow it will be my last. I prefer the company of my dog Amigo or even of Gustavo.

What can I say? I am a *misanthrope* in the literal sense of the term. Something is out of joint either with me or my society (or both), but it doesn't make any difference which one it is; the outcome is the same. I like to think that it is my society that is utterly corrupted; yet who knows, there may be something amiss with my own mental wiring. Writing all this down may not solve anything, but it does make me feel better. I could go on and on… but it is time to stop!

42

I like the word "soul." It is a good old English term that gets right to the essence of what I am usually thinking about. "Mind" is too intellectual, "spirit" too ecclesiastical, "psyche" too psychoanalytic, "self" is nondescript. "Soul" includes all the properties of these other terms plus some. Using it as an adjective, I am obliged to say "spiritual," but "soulish," if it did not sound comical, would be better. Unfortunately, the latter is not an accepted English word. It is too bad that the German *Geist* is not in English dictionaries. (Ghost is far off the mark.) Its adjectival forms, *geistig* and *geistlich*, separate the metaphysical meaning of spiritual from the ecclesiastical. Whenever I write "spiritual," I mean *geistig.*

* * *

It should be more widely known that many of the foremost scientists in neurophysiology have opted for the concept of "soul" (spirit, mind) existing within a different dimension of reality compared to the material brain. Sir Charles Sherrington, the father figure of British neurophysiology who won a Nobel Prize for his studies on the nervous system, concluded that there was nothing about the cellular structure of the human brain that could account for the higher mental functions of *Homo sapiens* (*Man on his Nature*). He admitted in the last introduction to his epoch-making book *Integrative Action of the Nervous System* that it was no more improbable that the human conditions should consist of two fundamental "elements" than of only one. Sherrington was not a dogmatic materialist.

One of Sherrington's students, Wilder Penfield, went on as a neurosurgeon to pioneer in direct studies of the human brain. He and his colleagues at the Montreal Neurological Institute mapped out brain correlates of mental and motor functions of human subjects. He went further than his mentor in asserting that the dualist hypothesis is the much more reasonable one for explaining the nature of the human mind (*The Mystery of the Mind*, 1975). Interestingly, the Nobel-winning physicist Erwin Schrödinger who was interested in biology had come to the same conclusion (*On the Peculiarity of the Scientific World-view*, 1956).

It irritates me when "neuropsychologists," "neurophilosophers," (a detestable term), and computer technicians are so dismissive of the idea that the soul is an element of the human condition distinct in nature from the brain. Most of these armchair dogmatists have never seen a human brain, much less subjected it to experimental studies. Yet the materialist dogma is very strong among the intelligentsia. It has done irreparable damage to human culture.

I don't know about the souls of neurophilosophers or neuropsychologists but I know that my soul is a metaphysical reality. If I did not have a soul to enrich my existence, my whole life would have been an absurd waste of energy.

43

A great deal of my life has been affected by an incorrigible *metaphysical need* that has never been satisfied, certainly not by traditional religions, and especially not by Christianity, which claims to possess universal truth. I am less conversant with eastern religions but my mind will never abandon the importance of personal development about which there is little emphasis in eastern metaphysical thought. Thus I am forced to fall back on my own resources for attempted satisfaction of my metaphysical need.

I don't ever expect to comprehend the entire universe, and am hoping that death, which at my age cannot be far off, will open new vistas for me.

* * *

Reading C.S. Lewis' *Mere Christianity*. It is quite a simplistic treatment of the Christian religion, but he does make one interesting point. God is commonly regarded as a universal "father" by all devout Christians. "Our Father who art in heaven," is the beginning of one of the holiest prayers in Christendom. This would seem to make the worshippers brothers to Christ. Lewis points out, however, that Christ is the *only begotten* son of God, whereas the rest of us were *created* by him and thus have a different type of relationship. With God, we are more like the relationship of sculpture to the sculptor.

But what if this dogma is incorrect? What if we are truly all begotten of God? Then Jesus of Nazareth is truly our brother. This seems more plausible because if an "event" happens only once, it is suspect; if it is recurrent, it is more likely to be a valid phenomenon. The Vedantic (Indian) doctrine "Atman is Brahman" means that all human beings have a potentially equal relationship to Deity.

44

The ancient Greek originators of philosophy were superior to anything in the English-language world of today that goes under the name of philosophy. Pythagoras, Heraclitus, Parmenides, Socrates, Diogenes of Sinope, Epicurus, Zeno, Pyrrho were genuine philosophers—"lovers of wisdom"—in every sense of the term. Their similarities, namely that they *lived out* their philosophies, is much more important than their doctrinal differences. Plato and Aristotle seem to me to have been of a different breed; Plato was a prolific *littérateur* initiating this tradition in philosophy while Aristotle was a forerunner of the "strict scientific" mentality of philosophy. I do not rank these latter two as high as the real "lovers of wisdom" of the antique Greek societies.

Finally, Christianity edged out all the Greek schools of philosophy and brought the metaphysical consciousness of the Mediterranean area to its lowest common denominator. The Greek philosophical schools that had originated serious metaphysical thinking generally did not indulge themselves in extravagant divagations from the contemporary religions of that time (Plato excluded, who set the stage for the later Christianity). Their philosophies were aimed at promoting thoughtful individuals, spiritually as well as materially. Today, one would do well to study them, not as dead history, but as models for contemporary thought.

No one can know anything of life after death, even if it may be reasonable to believe that the soul is not extinguished upon death of the body. But the metaphysical need of individuals should not be assuaged with the absurdities of religious imagination.

Metaphysics must not violate man's precious intellectual conscience. Furthermore, any person engaged in philosophical thought should heed the admonition of Diogenes of Sinope that a philosophy is worthless if it does not bite into people's illusions or otherwise disturb them.

45

The significance of art, literature, philosophy, and all the other spiritual manifestations of human beings is that they reveal human *creativity*. It is not the content of creative activity that is the most important; it is that individuals can be creative. This is what reveals the supernatural element within them. "God" is not the only creative force in the universe; his creations are also creative.

To be creative is necessarily to be subjective. The truths of subjectivity must be distinguished from the truths of objectivity, which are dependent on natural law and exist in a different realm of being. When Jesus of Nazareth said, "I am the truth," when Soren Kierkegaard said, "Truth is Subjectivity," and when Nicolas Berdyaev identified the free creative spirit as the most important aspect of the human condition, they were all referring in different ways to the distinguishing *creative* element of human beings.

This is what I believe.

46

Why do I write in this journal so assiduously? It is a question I often ask myself. There is no visible purpose I can identify, no goal that it might serve in my life. I do not expect anyone to read it except by some fluke after I am long gone. I not only compose this journal but I take great pains to make it into the best literary form of which I am capable. I transcribe the raw handwritten pages into my word processor, improving it all the while and then print it out even though I know that it won't be read by anyone except myself. Even more to the point, I honestly do not *wish* for any readers, which to me would be an intrusion into the intimacies of my soul.

Since there is no psychological or even physiological purpose to this activity, there must be some metaphysical one. I have finally uncovered the intuition that in writing this journal, *I am creating my own soul.* At the risk of descending into utter hubris, I will speculate that I write this journal for the same reason that God created the universe, except that I am creating my soul. It is an expression of the divinity in my nature, requiring care and precision. Since there will be no readers of it in my lifetime or likely any other time, I have no fear of ridicule or abusiveness by others. The more I reflect on my intuition, the truer it seems to me. My journal is the one important element in my life, which is why I put so much effort into it.

* * *

In the entry above, I somewhat glibly asserted the biblical idea that "God created the universe." I ought to defend this assertion. My defense is simple; my mind cannot conceive that the vast universe in which I live, with its natural laws, its phenomena of life, and its conscious beings such as myself could have come into existence without some purposeful external action. My mind could still stubbornly say it is theoretically possible, but it could not really accept the idea. It would violate my intellectual conscience. There must be a *creative force* responsible for the universe. I call this creative force "God" out of habit and for lack of a suitable substitute, without attributing to it any of the absurdities concocted by the Abrahamic religions.

47

An Article of Faith: By elevating my consciousness, I am elevating the consciousness of the Divinity (God). All creative beings are capable of continually elevating their consciousness and God should be no exception. Even if I cannot form any conception of how my own spiritual development acts to enrich God, I have come to believe that this must be the case. Individual human beings whose consciousness, i.e. spirituality, is elevated through learning, experience, and creative activity pass on their accomplishment to the ultimate metaphysical reality of the universe. This, I believe, is the purpose of the metaphysical development of *Homo sapiens.*

The common concept of Vedanta Hinduism, Buddhism, and Christianity is that the final goal of the soul of human beings should be to blend into the "absolute," the ultimate reality, the Christ-God. The terminology and rhetoric are different but the goals are the same. Whether it be the naïve heaven of Christianity, the more intellectual "Atman is Brahman" of Vedanta, or the Nirvana void of Buddhism, uniting with the Absolute Being is the goal. All the benefit is to the individual, none to the Absolute. The believer sacrifices his spiritual individuality. This is a limited, restrictive view of the man-god relationship. A more expansive view is needed—and justified in my humble opinion. *Homo sapiens* ought to move beyond the obsequious, slave-like attitude to Deity of religions where all that counts is obedience. Eating from the tree of knowledge of good and evil is not sin but is what has justified the continuation of mankind. It is a great thing to realize that one's own spiritual development has meaning in the larger scheme of things. Then the desire for immortality becomes a minor matter and the need for religion becomes superfluous. The mystical insight of Angelus Silesius can be then finally confirmed:

> *Ich weiss dass ohne mich Gott nicht ein Nu kann leben,*
> *Werd ich zu nicht, er muss von Not den Geist aufgeben.*
>
> —*Der cherubinischer Wandersmann*

> I know that God cannot live one instant without me,
> If I should come to naught, He must cease to be.

48

An Epiphany: After my last entry, a mystical insight arose in me indicating that my soul is really an *essential* extension of the reality of "God." The physical self with its sensory apparatus serves to grow one's soul, thereby enhancing God. When the physical self can no longer serve this purpose, it is discarded through its death. Experiences, learning, reflection, and creative writing is how the physical self grows the soul. So it seems as if my soul is growing but it is truer to say that God is growing through me.

This process is vouchsafed to me from God as a kind of investment He makes in a human being in order to enrich himself. "Investment" is an appropriate term. I am His investment. Through me and those like me, He rises to a richer level of existence. Thus God is not perfect but is in a state of constant perfecting through all the souls that contribute to Him. Every human being who has ever developed his spirituality has played a part in this process—some more than others.

The religions that have become institutionalized throughout history really represent failed efforts of God at self-realization. But possibly all the sins of Christianity are vindicated through the assertion in John 4:24, "God is a spirit." Once one apprehends this fundamental insight, things fall into place; the cosmos becomes comprehensible. An individual human being can only comprehend a small part of it; however, the smallest degree of comprehension serves to enrich God. In this process, every individual is as potentially significant as was Jesus Christ. It is a matter of developing consciousness of the meaning of *spirit* and realizing the subsidiary role played by *matter*. This was Christianity's great contribution to humanity, which serves to mitigate the corroding effects of its dogmas, authoritarianism, and cruelties. This is why scientism, in spite of its accomplishments, ends by having a destructive effect on the wellbeing of humanity.

49

I am not very good at describing Nature. A Senancour or a Wordsworth would be required to do justice to the natural beauty of the "mountain empire" in which I live in far southern Arizona. The huge sweep of the horizon enclosing grasslands, forests, foothills, mountains—nature's doings in every form, would be better served through visual art rather than by literary means. Especially grand are the vast skies with ever-changing cloud formations and spectacular sunsets displaying their hues of lavender and crimson. Every day and every evening are different as though some cosmic Creator is constantly experimenting with his palette. Not the least of its attractions is the absence of the urban blight that ruins everything.

However,… I know that all this beauty is really a product of my own mind. Descriptions of a physicist, geologist, or field biologist of nature would be quite different. The Apache Indians who lived here for centuries before being dispossessed by the westward march of Americans may or may not have noticed it to the degree that I do. Noticing beauty is an affair of spirit and requires spiritual consciousness. Where would this come from? Not from that ugly gray lump of gelatinous tissue in my cranial cavity. Not from all those tangled fibrous strands of nerve cells. Not from the biochemical or electrical peculiarities of these cells. It must come from my soul and ultimately the spiritual source I consent to call God—for want of a better name.

Like the gravitational force of the universe, there is a kind of "attraction" between God and the concentration of God-like spirit within me that I call my soul. However, this analogy should not be pushed very far as the nature of spiritual attraction must be far different than that of matter. No mathematical equations will ever encompass it. I have assimilated the thought of Angelus Silesius previously quoted to the effect that God cannot exist without me. Perhaps it is hyperbole, but it is meaningful all the same.

Dostoevsky wrote in his novel *The Idiot*, "Beauty will save the world." He surely must have meant the spiritual significance of beauty.

50

Living the isolated life that I do, I worry sometimes that I may be hurting my soul by dispensing with social contacts. I do not obtain the emotional and intellectual stimulation that I would through interchange with others. I do not have the "feed-back" that comes from others' opinions of my thoughts. But I believe that at this time in my life I am better off with solitude instead of interminable interactions. It is time for me to become independent of the world. I don't want to "overcome" it; I want not to need it for my wellbeing; I want not to be dragged down by it to an ever-diminishing quality of my existence.

In the beginning of my life, I was dependent on the womb, then dependent on my family during my childhood, later dependent on my youthful milieu. I must confess that I don't rate highly any of these dependencies. Then I entered into university teaching, but the quality of my milieu did not improve. The necessity of satisfying peers, superiors, or the public became intolerable to me. Whatever benefits I derived from these dependencies and relationships had been long exhausted. It was then that I decided to radically change my life. I gave up my university position and most of my possessions. I obtained a position in a small post office in southern Arizona in which minimal demands were made upon my mind. I was able to purchase a cabin at the edge of the Coronado National Forest. I embarked on a life of solitude.

It took some time, but eventually the spiritual potential within me began to emerge. My mind cleared, I appreciated nature, *I appreciated myself*. Like the great Emory oak tree near my cabin, my soul began to spread out. Instead of foreign influences constantly playing upon me, my own nature began to emerge. The direction of flow of my spirit reversed. At first, it was a creativity of thought; then it became a creativity of expression. I care little of what others think of the style or substance of my creativity; it is enough for me that it emerges from my own soul out into the world. The creativity comes from my own spiritual resources; i.e., from the divinity within me. I believe I am fulfilling my destiny as a human being.

I'm aware of the pejorative labels that could be attached to me were anyone to become interested in how I live my life. Narcissism, egocentricity, autism, sociopathy, megalomania, and finally insanity come to mind. At best, I could be dismissed as a harmless mystical dreamer. But all these would be just name-calling; I recall a childhood ditty, "Sticks and stones will break my bones but names will never hurt me." As long as I can maintain my level of basic sustenance, society's insults will not bother me. But I do not feel able, like Hindu *Sannyasins*, to wander about begging my bread. I need the small income to which I am entitled.

Instead of society, I have Divinity. The greatest thinkers of the world were of one mind in praising solitude. Petrarch, Rousseau, and Thoreau come to mind, but there are many others. I am fulfilling my contract with the ultimate metaphysical being of the universe. There is a mutual dependence between God and me. What time there is left for me in this life I want to utilize to enrich this relationship. I can *imagine* God outside of myself but I can only *experience* him within myself. But I do not consider myself a pantheist. I prefer the term coined by Karl Christian Krause, *panentheism*—an attitude that allows both God and myself to preserve our precious individuality.

51

The Russian philosopher Nicholas Berdyaev and the Spanish philosopher Miguel de Unamuno show remarkable similarities. Both wrote their hallmark works just prior to the First World War when Europe still thought itself to represent the epitome of civilization. Both were champions of spiritual reality and opponents of dogmatic scientism. Both professed allegiance to Christianity but ran afoul of the state churches in their native lands. Both might be classified as "existential" philosophers since they wrote from strongly personalized points of view. Both were exiled from their native lands because of their political or religious convictions: Unamuno temporarily but Berdyaev for the rest of his life. It is surprising that neither seemed to pay attention to the other although their time in Paris overlapped.

Berdyaev was facing exile to Siberia on charges of blasphemy from which he was spared because of the outbreak of the First World War. Unamuno's main writings were placed on the Roman Catholic Index of Forbidden Books. Yet, curiously, in spite of their devastating criticisms of the established Christian churches, neither of them abandoned their identity as Christians and both considered themselves to be faithful to Christianity throughout their lives.

Why was this so? They both knew that untold misery and suffering had been inflicted on the peoples of Europe and elsewhere under the banner of the Church militant. They were aware of the evils of religious authoritarianism. They were quite capable of assimilating the significant spiritual elements of historical Christianity without subscribing to a doctrinaire religion. They could have become fully independent as spiritual figures without carrying a label that confused their philosophies and exposed them to unnecessary contradictions. Yet they did not ever do so.

I attribute their persistence in hanging on to the Christian identity to their fear that abandoning it would compromise their spirituality. There is much spiritual tradition associated with the Christian faith. "Liberal" folk living under the sign of scientism do not have this fear since they have weak or nil spiritual consciousness. But Berdyaev and Unamuno were committed to the spiritual element of their existence. They believed in the significance of their souls. Giving up their traditional connections with their national Christianities was too difficult for them.

Coming from a Jewish ancestry, I do not have that problem. Being spiritual and being Christian have not been indelibly fused in my mind from childhood. Quite the contrary, I grew up thinking of Christians as potentially dangerous, violent people. It was only later that I learned of the spiritual element of the Christian religion. Thus it has been easy for me to strive toward spiritual consciousness without the imprimatur of a Christian connection.

52

From Friedrich Nietzsche's notebooks of 1885:

> "In this era, where hoi polloi (*der Pöbel*) rules and awards honors, it is more unworthy of philosophers to crave them than in any previous age."

So I justified my abandonment of the search for academic success. As far as my writings and the public are concerned, my permanent motto is *attrape qui peut*, which may be idiomatically translated as "catch as catch can."

From the same notebook:

> "Germany, which is so rich in clever and capable scholars, has lacked for a long time great souls, mighty spirits—to such an extent that it appears to have forgotten what is a *great* soul, what is a *mighty* spirit."

Instead of Germany, one could without loss of pertinence substitute the United States of America. English-language philosophers have exiled themselves to the ivory tower materialist mentality of their academic institutions to the point where no one knows who they are or what purpose they serve.

53

The desire has come upon me to express who and what I am—mainly to remind myself, but also to enlighten any adventurous individual who might read this journal some day. I was raised quite uneventfully in upper Manhattan by adoptive parents. I thought I had been born in New York City, but much later I discovered my birthplace was in Byelorussia and I had been brought to America at five years of age. My father who was quite resourceful in such things arranged for me to obtain a birth certificate from New York. At that time, this was possible for not much money. My parents who had both taught at a Russian university in Minsk were fluent in English, which was the only language that was spoken to me at home. When they wished that I not understand something they were discussing, they spoke in Russian or rarely in Yiddish. Actually my mother was Russian and didn't like it when my father occasionally lapsed into his childhood tongue. He was a nonobservant Jew who had only contempt for ignorant Rabbis and the Orthodox Jewish way of life. His hero was Bertrand Russell. Both my parents worked, leaving me in the care of a German-Jewish nanny whose main contribution to my development was learning German. Her civilized family members were early refugees from Nazi Germany; I still remember her fulminating against Adolf Hitler, "*Dass Ignorant! Dass Gesindel!* He is destroying German culture, the

German spirit!" Unfortunately, she was right. Even worse, he turned out to be a madman who, besides the Jews of Europe, almost destroyed all Germany.

I was an excellent student and obtained top grades at Stuyvesant High School, the crème de la crème of Manhattan public high schools. My father had high hopes for an academic career for me, but fate decreed otherwise for a time. World War II broke out when I was sixteen years old. Most of my friends were filled with patriotic ardor and couldn't wait to enlist. I had to delay a while until I came of age and then promptly enlisted in the Army. It was the greatest day of my young life. But I had no real knowledge of what I was getting into. Although I was a clever student, I was extremely immature and naïve.

The first year of my military life was filled with boredom, restlessness, and the realization that I was not cut out for army life. I never got past private first class. Being transferred to England was interesting for a time, but then came Omaha Beach. I was confronted with the frightening reality of death, my death. Wading onto the beach in the midst of constant shelling and machine gun fire, soldiers dying all around me, some of them my friends, panic-stricken, not knowing what to do or where to go to escape the carnage; it was by far the most fearful experience of my life. I developed a facial tic that has not left me to this day.

But I survived. Ultimately, my platoon was reconstituted and when the Germans finally gave way in Normandy, we began our drive through northern France. I was part of Patton's Third Army, whose reputation for lightening advances became a legend. The German Army seemed to have lost its capacity to resist. German soldiers were surrendering in droves. Now I have to relate something that I have never fully faced myself—never mind telling anyone else.

My platoon was required to move fast over rough country roads. We had absolutely no way of taking prisoners, either guarding them or feeding them. Our lieutenant could not tolerate leaving enemy soldiers behind our advancing column. There were rumors of loose soldiers raiding supply dumps and attacking ambulances. So we shot to death weaponless Germans who had surrendered with their hands raised high. I did not set the policy, but I participated in it. They were probably the only Germans I ever killed: how many I don't remember. Whether other platoons or companies did the same, I can't say. I only know what we did, what I did.

This memory has been as traumatic for me as Omaha Beach. It is a terrible feeling to know you have killed unresisting young men. I have wondered why I did not hold back from the murder—for that is what it was—but at that time in my life I was incapable of such independent behavior. Perhaps, even though I was young, it revealed a lack of character that I have to live with. I think this memory has produced a permanent sense of foreboding in me and a pessimism, often unpleasantly cynical, that along with my facial tic will never leave me.

54

The War ended and I was demobilized. The traumas of combat receded into my subconscious and I slowly began to pick up the threads of my life. I enrolled at the City College of New York, which was then a center of both student and faculty intellectual activity. My father thought I should enroll as a premedical student but I soon found that my inclinations led me in a different direction—toward philosophy. I fell in love with philosophy as an undergraduate student, a love that has never left me. There was one charismatic professor of philosophy at CCNY, a former student of the eminent German "existentialist" philosopher Karl Jaspers, who inspired me to seek to make a profession of philosophy. The GI Bill permitted me to engage in graduate studies at New York University without depending on financial support from my family.

As part of my graduate work, I spent two years at the Sorbonne in Paris. Those were halcyon days in my life. I came into contact with Sartre and the other mandarins of existentialism in the cafés of St. Germain. To tell the truth, I was not greatly taken by the great man himself. The exaggerated intellectualism of the heroes of French philosophy at that time always seemed too *recherché* or too political for my taste. I prefer more truly existential types like Nietzsche, Unamuno, and Berdyaev. But the atmosphere was exceptionally stimulating for a young man and strengthened my commitment to philosophy. A considerable fringe benefit was that I became quite comfortable reading and writing French.

When I returned to New York, I devoted myself to completing my graduate studies and finishing my dissertation on Goethe's contribution to German philosophical idealism. Finally, in my early thirties, I received my Ph.D. and began to seriously think about a career for myself. Then began my disillusionment with philosophy as a career.

The GI Bill was at an end for me. My parents had both died. The only remunerative position I could obtain would be as an instructor at the bottom rung of some college or university. There were many more applicants than positions in philosophy, besides the fact that there were many highly qualified English-speaking Europeans who were anxious to leave the devastation of postwar Europe for a job in affluent America. The competition was intense. Finally, I obtained a position at a small college in Pennsylvania whose name I shall refrain from mentioning. Besides teaching Introduction to Philosophy and Logic, I was required to teach courses in Classics and another in Ancient History for which I was not at all prepared.

There was the drudgery of preparing lectures, marking papers, and assigning grades—tasks that interested me not at all. But beyond these chores, I discovered I was not a natural-born teacher. I was much more interested in the substance of philosophy than in teaching it to students, most of whom were taking it as a snap subject to fulfill their course requirements. Philosophy was easier than Physics or Calculus. My personality was such that I did not relate easily to young immature students. Fortunately for me, the practice of grading instructors by students had not yet entered into higher education. Otherwise, my academic career would have ended earlier than was the case.

It did not take long, however, for a more serious problem to emerge. This was the question of obtaining tenure. It was not just that tenure protected one from arbitrary dismissal; it was that if tenure were not obtained within a certain period, dismissal was *mandatory*. It can hardly be surprising that obtaining tenure has been the number one concern of junior faculty for a very long time in the American university system. How does one obtain tenure? It is very simple: one must publish in peer-reviewed professional journals. Even better, one should publish books. There are other routes to tenure in the sciences, but for philosophy, the oft-quoted maxim "publish or perish" holds true.

With respect to the above, yet another difficulty existed for me. My natural interests were in what is loosely called "continental" philosophy or existentialism, i.e., philosophy based on immediate intuitions rather than on the model of the sciences. But American philosophy is entirely devoted to this latter variety, which may also be characterized as "analytic" philosophy. The type of papers I submitted for publication was thrown out of court by American philosophy journals. The only thing I could do that would be acceptable was to write accounts or critiques of important figures in philosophy. But I was not interested in being an historian or critic; I wanted to be a *philosopher.*

The sum and substance of it all was that after six years of vainly trying to swim against adverse currents, I abruptly resigned my position. I relocated to a remote area in the southwest, as far as I could get from the more traditional eastern part of the country. I obtained a government job in a small local post office in order to support myself while giving myself the mental freedom to pursue my own course.

55

A whole new life opened up for me in far southern Arizona. My position at the post office, while requiring regular attendance, left me with a completely free mind during my working hours. I was able to think in *freedom.* T. S. Eliot wrote somewhere that a post office was ideal employment for a poet since it did not divert his mind from poetical creativity. The same is true and even more so for a philosopher. The material world does not weigh heavily on one when he is a post office employee.

I have said nothing about my relationships with the other sex but they have been a factor in my life since puberty. Women have always attracted me, not merely for the purpose of isolated sex (although that too), but as erotic *soulmates*. Plato's conception of the perpetual search for one's missing half has seemed perfect to explain my condition regarding the opposite sex. Twice I entered into marital relationships but, like my university career, the conjugal role was not suited for me. Also, not having much money complicated everything. The metaphysical elements of an erotic relationship soon evaporated under the pressures of bourgeois life. I do not intend to reveal any details of my intimate relationships since they do not belong in a journal. Suffice it to say that my marriages ended in regrets but with relief on my part.

I worked at the post office for over twenty years, long enough to qualify for a small pension. I reflected for a long time on how I should live after retirement. I decided what I needed most was *solitude*, real solitude, not the temporary or make-believe monastic type. I had the intuition that only in this way could my true self emerge and flourish. The few people I knew shook their heads when they heard of my intention and did not hesitate to tell me I was deluding myself. But never being much affected by the opinions of others, I went ahead with my plans.

When I had left my college position, I had received a lump sum of money from my contributions to a pension plan. Miraculously, I had held on to this nest egg during my time at the post office. This enabled me to buy a small cottage (really a cabin) adjacent to the Coronado National Forest and near the Mexican border. It was almost totally isolated, except for Border

Patrol vehicles passing by periodically or, rarely, hunters or adventurers. I possessed an old Jeep that allowed me to obtain provisions or mail at a crossroads community quite a few miles away. It was perfect for my purposes. All I had to connect me to the wider world was a laptop that operated in slow motion. Thus I entered into a new phase of my existence.

56

I have often recapitulated to myself why I have chosen a solitary life. Is it that I recognize that the nature of the social systems within my society bear down too heavily on my soul, that I am fundamentally a metaphysical creature living within a fundamentally materialist environment, or that I am as alienated from it as if I were a visitor from the planet Mars? The economic colonialism of the United States is not merely pressed down upon other countries of the world, but also upon its own peoples. Relentless intrusive commercialism in America is a subtle variety of colonialism. Insidious and sometimes blatant invasion into one's psyche by the ubiquitous electronic screens that is part of American life undermines one's spiritual development. Solitary life for me is a form of self-defense against the weight of an intrusiveness crushing my spirit. Alone, I have space to breathe freely and make something of my inner self.

I feel my solution to the problem of living in America is appropriate at this moment in time for me. I do not speak for others or even for myself if the time and place were different. But they are what they are and I have embraced the fate that I have chosen for myself. *Amor fati* was Nietzsche's answer to a similar predicament in which he found himself. The fact that he was not able to live up to his solution does not mean it was not the correct one. I have made a commitment to a solitary life as the best way to develop my soul and I have accepted whatever consequences may flow from it.

57

Philosophy is either intuitional (mystical) or rational (logical). Both forms of thinking determine a philosopher's beliefs; however, one or the other is usually dominant. Much depends on one's background and education but ultimately it is a matter of the temperament of the philosopher. England equally produced a Bertrand Russell and a D.H. Lawrence (the latter was more interested in philosophy than story-telling). The two greatest Spanish philosophers of the twentieth century were Miguel de Unamuno and José Ortega y Gasset, who were the most opposite of types.

In general, though, the English-language culture produces analytic, scientifically-minded professional logicians while the European continent tends to produce metaphysically-minded philosophers. French philosophy is more intellectual than intuitional although it does not ignore metaphysics. Russian thought has been much more spiritual than the rest of Europe—the Communist era was an aberration. However, all these generalizations are disputable as the most strictly descriptive phenomenologists in the end have a metaphysical soul that motivates their "science."

I consider myself to be primarily an intuitional type who utilizes logic and rationality only to support my point of view. In this I am akin to the medieval scholastics who lived by the maxim *fides quaerens intellectum* (faith in search of understanding), except my "faith" is not in the revelations of an almighty God but is a trust in the insights of my own soul.

When I write, I just don't pour out my soul like a Kerouac or a Strindberg (the latter said he did not dare to change any of his writing). I dare; I look for *le mot juste.* I look to create esthetic and sculptural qualities in my writing and I try to incorporate new insights. It gives me great pleasure when I think I am successful. My creative spirit is *artistic.* Not *l'art pour l'art* but art for my soul. I never imagine readers other than myself for my writings.

* * *

At my age, I am increasingly possessed by awareness of the approach of a *tragic* end to my individuality. Everything living must die, but only humans have an awareness of this necessity. Leaving behind traces and memories of my present existence does not mitigate the feeling of tragedy in me. The posthumous remains of writings, achievements, photographs, children (hypothetical)—none of these lessen in any way my feeling that I am destined for a tragic end. I find temporary pleasures in creative activity or in emotional and physical gratifications; these pleasures keep my mind and body alive but do not eliminate the tragic awareness that is part of my consciousness. I know the relentless deterioration of my body necessitates its end, but this only sharpens its tragic nature.

Whatever will be the fate of my soul, it will not replace what it is today. Whatever transfiguration may occur to it will not substitute for my present hard-won individuality. There is no escaping the tragedy other than acceptance of fate in a manner worthy of a philosopher. The gifted Portuguese writer Fernando Pessoa is reported to have sadly said in his stilted English on the day of his death, "I know not what the morrow will bring." This is how I feel about the morrow that is yet to come for me.

58

My library occupies the better part of my cabin; much of it will not fit anywhere and remains in boxes not easily available to me. Contemplating it, beginning with Heraclitus up to the present era, the feeling overwhelms me at times that everything worth saying has been said *ad infinitum*. As the Teacher of Ecclesiastes said, "What has been done will be done again; there is nothing new under the sun. Is there anything of which one can say, 'Look! This is something new? It was here already long ago, before our time.'" And more disturbingly, the antique commentator on Ecclesiastes ends by saying, "Of making many books there is no end, and much study is a weariness of the flesh." All this some 2,500 years ago.

Why write more books, which is merely tweaking or diminishing what has already been written? There could be a hundred-year moratorium on book publishing that would help conserve the environment and would be no loss to the universe of literature. People would go back to read what has already been written and make allowances for archaic styles of writing. It ought to be realized that publishing is an industry providing employment to many individuals and there would be some dislocations to be dealt with by the government. But publishing should not be a make-work activity similar to the civilian conservation core of the thirties in the U.S. or the men still pumping gasoline at *gasolineras* in Mexico. As far as contemporary authors are concerned, the Teacher of Ecclesiastes again seems to have the final wisdom. "Vanity of vanities," he says, "all is vanity!"

But I believe the Teacher is not expressing the whole truth. There is a deeper reason for creativity in any form, including writing. This reason is *creating the soul of the creator.* Every creative individual knows how much he or she has benefitted from creative activity. The soul of a creative person is deepened, enlarged, *enriched* by his work. No matter how exhausted the creative process leaves its creator, he knows in his depths that he is a broader and better person for it. Conversely, not bringing into fruition what is inside one is a tragedy for the individual and the world. Even beyond one's own self, every developed soul enriches the reality of the cosmos. Only a little mystical awareness is necessary to come to the realization of this latter truth.

The drive to creative activity is of the same order but higher than the drive to survival or to procreation. It is the spiritual self that dominates here rather than the physical self or the species. In spite of the wisdom of much of what the Teacher said, there *is* something new and special appearing in every writing done in a creative spirit, albeit it is not always easy to identify. This is reason enough for writing a new book.

* * *

In the realm of creative philosophy, all philosophers write from an immediate mystical or a discursive rational perspective. Almost always there is a mixture of the two, with one or the other dominant. Plato and Aristotle are still the best representatives of these two poles. The temperament of a reader will determine which he prefers. The idea of the Roman Catholic Church that a philosopher like Thomas Aquinas was in virtual possession of absolute philosophic truth is simply absurd and has been responsible for the intellectual decay of the Church. Perspectivism, pluralism, pragmatism, relativism are the various terms describing the right approaches in evaluating philosophies—an approach incomparably advocated by William James, professor at Harvard University for many years. (Harvard has not seen his like since.) Aquinas, Spinoza, Kant, Hegel, Schopenhauer, Nietzsche, Aurobindo, Bergson, Whitehead, Berdyaev, Schain, Khashaba, and many, many forgotten others in many, many obscure places all have had their own important contributions to make to *philosophia perennis*, none of which can ever have a legitimate claim to be *the truth*.

59

Toward the end of every year, I am reminded that the Christmas season reflects the bankruptcy of American culture in which consumerism and materialism run amok. Children are infected with these plagues at an early age. I don't have the literary skills to describe the disgusting desecration of a holiday supposedly celebrating the birth of the Savior but any perceptive observer cannot fail to be aware of its hypocrisy.

The birthday of the ascetic figure of Jesus of Nazareth, the greatest prophet in the history of Judaism and the supreme spiritual symbol of Christianity, has been perverted to serve the interests of commercialism. It is the same everywhere in the Christian world but it is at its worst in America. None of the pillars of society dare to seriously criticize the practice because the American economy depends upon Christmas sales. What would "business" be without them? Thus the absurdities of Christmas grow more flagrant every year and it seems that only the collapse of American civilization would be capable of getting rid of them.

However, outstanding societies have prospered without the commercialism of Christmas. What is needed is a rebellion of the people against the corrupting influence of the profit motive in religion and a willingness to accept the economic consequences of a radical change in the economic structure of America.

60

I have a print of a portrait of Amadeo Modigliani entitled "Woman with Black Cravat." I can look at her youthful, delicate, pensive face for hours on end. I also have a copy of a nude painting of Modi's that I am sure is of the same model in which the splendor of her body is fully revealed. Perhaps one day she will step out of her portrait and embrace me. We will make love. It is just as well that my fantasy will never come true because the reality could not come up to my expectations. The sad fact is that the shy intense youth of yesteryear still lives within my aging body. Well I am a dreamer and I get great pleasure from my dreams.

61

Aristotle in the *Metaphysics* says that it is "owing to their wonder" that men began to philosophize. This was an unusual remark for Aristotle who was not given to exaggeration or flowery statements. He recognized, however, that philosophy was associated with a special state of consciousness that he called "wonder." Other predicates could be applied, but basically I prefer to think philosophy is the outcome of a certain *spiritual* state of mind seeking expression. As soon as one begins to analyze this state of mind, however, the spiritual element evaporates. Rational analysis and spiritual consciousness are not compatible mental states. One can alternate with the other but this usually leads to a diminishing quality of one or both states as can be seen in scholastic philosophy where rationality usually outshines spirituality. It is ironic that no one was guiltier of removing the wonder from philosophy than Aristotle himself with his unremitting analytic approach to it.

An analytic mindset is useful for securing and promoting human life but it is the death of the spiritual state. Philosophy elevates consciousness of an individual but provides no solution of the concrete problems of an individual. The development of philosophical systems may sharpen the mind of the philosopher as would crossword puzzles or foreign language study, but a searcher for wisdom gains nothing from philosophical systems unless, as was the case with Spinoza and Schopenhauer, the soul of the philosopher can be discerned behind their systems. Regarding "cognitive science" or any other philosophy scientifically-conceived, these belong in the domain of science—except without verification of empirical *data*, they cannot obtain the approval of authentic scientists.

When Jesus was asked by his admirers to prove his spiritual claims by performing miracles, he very properly resisted and did so only under duress. The role of a prophet, which is a category of philosophy, is to elevate consciousness, not to perform miracles. Today, miracles have been replaced by scientific achievements in which most contemporary philosophers would love to participate. Unfortunately for them, they have no capacity for scientific study so that they end being neither philosopher nor scientist. More often than not, they turn to politics for which they have even less capacity.

The fundamental problem of philosophy today is that it is largely confined to academic institutions in which spiritual consciousness carries very little weight. Academic philosophers have to *perform*; they have to publish, gain publicity, obtain peer recognition, and even, like scientists, get grants of money. They are more akin to certain antique sophists rather than to philosophers in the Socratic model. Above all, their values do not include metaphysical consciousness, except insofar as they may use metaphysical subjects for doctoral dissertations or scholarly publications.

The linguistic derivation of the antique Greek term *philosophia* is "love of wisdom." *Wisdom* is not erudition, critical thinking, or scholarly prowess; it is an elevated state of mind with respect to the human condition. Funk and Wagnall's dictionary lists 23 synonyms for wisdom with almost as many antonyms attesting to the difficulty of definition of this word. The emergence of wisdom in an individual is a great mystery but its judicious use is the main element in philosophical expression. Devout Christians believe that wisdom is a function of revelation originating from the Christian God but this is no more than a speculation, usually confined to fundamentalists or professional clergy. These folk are inclined to view divine revelation as a message about the will of God, an idea that is quite bizarre in my judgment… but I am digressing from my subject.

Alfred North Whitehead made the following astounding statement, considering that he was the doyen of scientific philosophy in the twentieth century and the mentor of Bertrand Russell:

> "The universe shows us two aspects: on one side it is physically wasting, on the other side, it is spiritually ascending. It is thus passing…to new conditions, amid which the physical world, as we at present know it, will be represented by a ripple barely to be distinguished from non-entity."
>
> —*Religion in the Making*, 1926 (final page)

Shades of Hegel and dualism! This intuitive assertion of Whitehead justifies the emphasis placed by Schain on the centrality of the soul in human existence. As yet, however, there is no evidence that the concept of soul has escaped the stigma of superstition in our world dominated by scientism.

62

I believe in approaching the problems affecting belief in the soul in an orderly manner. First of all, there are the Christian legends. It is not necessary to accept the doctrines of ascent of virtuous souls to heaven or descent of sinful ones to hell to believe that human beings have a soul. Nor is it necessary to believe in the immortality of individual souls, although their persistence after death is a viable possibility. These naïve doctrines date from the beginning of Christianity when it was necessary to provide incentives for converting the pagan population of the Roman Empire. They can be discarded without affecting the compelling intuition of every individual that his soul is the central feature of his existence.

The dogmas of scientism require a little more careful attention. Monistic materialism can be defined as the dogma that anything truly existent can be sensed, directly or with instrumentation, and measured quantitatively. This limits the real world to matter and energy. Anything outside this definition is said to be superstition or illusion. "Souls" that cannot be sensed or measured belong to this category. All functions formerly attributed to the soul can be assumed by the brain with its apparently endless connectivity of neurons and its volatile electrical rhythms. The material brain produces mental activity; that is all one needs to know about spirit. The idea of an independent soul has become a dead letter—only utilized by poets or religious fundamentalists. The amazing success of the sciences in dominating nature has provided the ground on which these dogmas have rested.

However, the development of quantum mechanics has shaken the traditional worldview of materialism since it has called into question the nature of matter and its distinction from energy. Microphysics has revealed a difficulty in exactly defining the position and borders of "hard" matter. What used to be thought of as the corpuscular nature of matter seems to be untenable as the corpuscles receded further and further from instrumental view. Their borders can no longer be clearly defined but are more wavelike than precise. Furthermore, the old distinction between matter and energy no longer holds. Matter seems to more resemble packets of energy (quanta) than solid substance. Matter is convertible to the force of energy as the atomic bomb revealed in a terrifying manner. If the distinction between matter and energy is so blurred, the distinction between matter and spirit—spirit conceived as a transfiguration of energy by an admittedly bold conceptual leap—may also become blurred.

The development of mathematical physics and the emergence of its fantastic instrumentation has converted physics into an esoteric science incomprehensible to the public at large. The old belief of Heraclitus in a "logos common to all" is a dead letter in the present world of physics. It illustrates Heraclitus' other observation that "most men live as though their thinking were a private possession." The soul whose reality is dependent on metaphysical intuition has not yet made its appearance in microphysics. But when the furthest extension of the latter announces through "string theory" the existence of many more dimensions of reality than the conventional four, one might begin to wonder if the discovery of a "spiritual dimension" is not far off. Then might appear the reconciliation of metaphysics with science, envisioned by F. C. S. Schiller (*Riddles of the Sphinx,* 1910). Yet these are probably idle thoughts since the nature of spiritual energy must be qualitatively different from physical energy. As long as microphysics depends on quantitative physical data for its insights, these will never be relevant to the realm of spirit.

The most difficult problem for those who maintain the metaphysical nature of the soul is the compelling evidence that consciousness, a fundamental quality of the soul, is dependent on functioning of the brain. As stated earlier, if there is no activity in the brain, there is no visible consciousness in an individual. A dead person appears without a soul for all intents and purposes. One should keep in mind it is survivors that make this judgment; one can say nothing about possible internal feelings of a "brain-dead" person, unavailable to the survivors. For many, however, the stark impact of death is proof positive of the material nature of what is called the soul, even if the details of its anatomy and physiology have not yet been worked out by science. In the nineteenth century, the mechanical man-made robots depicted in literary form by the imaginations of Mary Shelley and Heinrich Heine craved souls for fulfillment, but did not know how to obtain them. This would not be the case today; science-minded people now believe that if they have a functioning brain, nothing more is needed for a fulfilling life.

Thoughts generated by brain activity are usually conceived of as a production process; the brain produces thought as the stomach produces acid or the kidneys urine. This concept was sharply critiqued quite a long time ago by William James in his essay *Human Immortality* (more focused on the brain-mind relationship rather than immortality *per se*), but his observations still hold true. It should be read by anyone interested in these problems. A *production* process is not the only way the brain can be related to thought; an alternative is a *transmission* process. The brain can function as a control station directing incoming and outgoing traffic (stimuli and responses) to their appropriate physical or spiritual destinations. A level of consciousness is associated with this process; if the control station does not function, consciousness disappears. However, the actual thoughts, emotions, and volitions are a function of one's soul, which can be envisioned as a concentration of spiritual energy. The physical body with its control center in the brain is thus a transmission mechanism allowing interaction of the soul of the individual with the world about him. Death destroys this mechanism and the spiritual energy presumably returns from whence it came. The spiritual reservoir of the universe must then do without the enrichment deriving from the independent position of the living person's soul.

This concept—and it is of course a concept, an alternative to the production theory of thought and the idea of soul as epiphenomenon—still does not explain how metaphysical reality interacts with the material reality of the brain. It is more than a century since William James reported the response of an eminent Berlin neurophysiologist to this dilemma: "*ignoramus, ignorabilimus*" was the answer; "we do not know, we will never know." It may be centuries from now that that answer will still be valid. However, the concept of transmission moves the origin of mental activity from the brain to the soul. This is a great advance in the conception of the human condition.

63

Philosophy is an art form like portrait or landscape painting. It depicts the linguistic response of the philosopher to his surrounding world. There must be attention to composition, detail, technique, and coherence. The finished product must bear some resemblance to the subject portrayed by the philosopher, but principally it must reveal his vision of and feeling about the world. Philosophy is art, not science. The scientist observes, describes, measures, and theorizes; the philosopher sees, intuits, feels, and expresses.

* * *

The "philosophical" analogue to mathematical physics is linguistic *analysis*. But whereas the former is based upon measurable, verifiable observations, linguistic theory is entirely spun out of the minds of linguists. They reject the idea of a common spiritual *logos* underlying human linguistic interactions; they require extensive analysis of language to determine its different meaning for different individuals. Thus an esoteric jargon has been developed analogous to that of mathematical physics in its incomprehensibility to the uninitiated. Like all unscientific jargons, it is largely composed of trivialities. At the dawn of the twentieth century, F. C. S. Schiller, the *enfant terrible* of Oxford philosophy from a former time, wrote that philosophy should be "a subject gentlemen can read with pleasure" (Preface to *Humanism: Philosophical Essays,* 1903). How far philosophy is now removed from that archaic thought! Even if one substitutes "individuals with a broad liberal education" for the term "gentlemen," the barbarous jargons of philosophy today cannot be read with comprehension, never mind with pleasure.

* * *

Philosophy, unlike science, *is* metaphysics. Until Ralph Waldo Emerson's essay on metaphysics entitled *Oversoul* (Essays 1st Series, 1846) is recognized as an important milestone in American philosophy and metaphysics in general is taken seriously, American university philosophy is destined to be trapped in the backwaters of a sterile scholasticism, without relevance to the human condition of the philosopher himself or of the world at large.

64

The eminent philosopher Henri Bergson once commented that any philosopher worth his salt has *one* idea that drives him forward. Kierkegaard said the same in his essay *Purity of Heart is to Will One Thing*. My one idea is the reality of the soul. I think the current decline of the human condition in western societies is due to loss of belief in the reality of the soul. It is not enough to have animal spirits, have Christian piety, be compassionate, be erudite or powerful in the world. One must first and foremost have reverence for one's own soul with all the implications that follow therewith. The needs of the soul must be fulfilled; otherwise one's human life is bound to be a failure. Eastern religions put the emphasis on tranquility of the soul but active fulfillment is more important no matter how much stress is generated. But no one can move toward spiritual fulfillment if they are not conscious of the soul's existence and its centrality in their life.

Nietzsche expressed his conception of spiritual fulfillment in *Thus Spoke Zarathustra* in the concept of the *"Übermensch,"* best translated as "superior person" (not superman or overman!).

But he did not describe the pathway from *Untermensch* to *Übermensch.* It may have been a chance mutation. Bergson, previously mentioned, felt that spiritual fulfillment was a consequence of creative evolution—the forward drive of an *élan vital.* This mystical conception caused him to be ostracized by the guild of academic philosophers, who to a man are committed to a faith in materialistic monism. Since Bergson, no philosopher in the academic world has dared to explicitly express "mystical" views.

65

Hindu Vedanta conceives of "Brahman" as the metaphysical reservoir of the soul. Atman equals Brahman is shorthand for this concept, bypassing the intermediary of the physical brain. Devout Vedantists are not interested in any role for the human body and prefer to concentrate on spiritual realities. They miss the point that the soul could not emerge without the input of physical sensory systems. Souls do not develop if individuals are forever locked in closets.

Perhaps the most pressing metaphysical question today is what happens to the soul upon death of the body. There are various possibilities proposed:

Evaporation into thin air upon death. This is the "epiphenomenon" explanation of materialists.

Return in some mysterious way to Brahman. The Vedanta view or Buddhist view for special individuals (entry into Nirvana).

Metempsychosis—migration into another living creature, human or animal. An ancient Hindu belief.

Transfiguration into a different dimension of reality. Analogous to the transfiguration of a caterpillar into a butterfly, but naturally more complex.

Choice 4 seems most likely to me, but the last word should be given to Heraclitus, "One cannot know or even imagine what happens to the soul after death." Whatever it may be, it will be completely different from its terrestrial life—just as the life of a butterfly is vastly different from that of a caterpillar.

The Teacher of Ecclesiastes who said, "all are of dust and all turn to dust again" (Eccl. 3:20) was a pessimistic materialist as are many today. This scion of King David did not apprehend the possibility of a radical transformation of his soul. It remained for a later prophet of Israel to proclaim that spiritual transfiguration occurs after death of an individual. He taught that souls go through the fires of terrestrial existence in order to become exalted in a new dimension of being.

* * *

Petrarch, perhaps the greatest mind of the Renaissance, thought the men of antiquity to be greater than those of his day.

Nietzsche was sure the powerful men of the Renaissance were far superior to those of his pedantic age. Schain thinks the philosophical minds of the nineteenth century had more depth than those of today. I suspect all those individuals were correct in their assessments and that mankind as we know it is on a downward course that may end spiritually in an ant age or in complete extinction. The great days of human beings may well be over. Nevertheless, "the future is not ours to tell...."

66

Anyone observing my life could not help noticing the huge discrepancy between my position in society and the audacious mental activity in which I engage. Kierkegaard commented on the vast theoretical castle constructed by the philosopher Hegel and the meager life he lived as a man. At least Hegel had recognition as a philosopher. My castle of thought is entirely subjective—it has no objective existence in the contemporary world.

So be it. I justify this discrepancy by claiming that my writings *develop my soul.* One developed soul is worth 10,000 undeveloped ones, to paraphrase Heraclitus. As recompense for my lack of recognition, I have my undisturbed solitude. I totally endorse the well-known dictum of Epicurus, "Live unknown."

If society had more to offer me, I might feel differently. If I had lived in Concord, Massachusetts in the 1830s and 40s among the Transcendentalists, in the mystical St. Petersburg of the last years of Czarist Russia, or in the vibrant ferment of interwar Paris, I might feel differently. But I don't; I live in a society in which the spiritual element is quite suffocated by materialism and scientism.

So I live in cultural and intellectual isolation. It seems to me that the most visionary thinkers of the Western world have recommended the virtues of the solitary existence. Petrarch, Montaigne, Rousseau, Nietzsche, and Robinson Jeffers all advised solitude for personal development. Like young plants, youth needs fertilization and frequent watering from without, but in time the more developed soul flourishes best when it becomes self-sufficient, only dependent on its own natural resources. The flow from *out to in* is reversed and becomes from *in to out*. Receptivity gives way to expressiveness. The basic need of mature plants for earth, water, sun, and air is paralleled for the soul by select books and rare human interactions. However, too much humanity is like too much fertilizer for plants; it is detrimental to spiritual development.

My era might be called the Age of Communication (worse yet, Social Networking). Solitude is looked upon with suspicion or contempt. The remarkable tools for communicating become more amazing every day. Yet the soul can only realize its highest potential in solitude, free from external distractions. This insight is absent in the modern world—largely because there is no consciousness of the existence of the metaphysical soul.

Is there any meaning, any purpose to what Balzac called *La Comédie Humaine*? In an effort to combat pessimism about humanity, one can speculate that the purpose is to create a few superior human beings: Übermenschen, Bodhisattvas, geniuses, saints who will populate a dimension of reality radically different than that of "hoi polloi." Nature is profligate in her disregard of most of her creations; the "earth mother" is really an evil stepmother who kills off most of her offspring and allows only a few favored ones to flourish. No idea could be more politically incorrect at the present time than this one, but this may be why it contains a large measure of truth.

* * *

I am now approaching eighty years of age, but this is my moment. Conditions have finally jelled for me to achieve the peak of my potential development as a philosopher. There must be a *meaning* to this accomplishment even though it has not been given to me to know it.

67

Schopenhauer said in one of his insightful essays that reading is thinking with another person's brain. This is especially true of philosophical reading. No doubt it is better than not thinking at all but still, it has its limitations. Every real philosopher creates his own unique *Weltanschauung* according to his temperament and intellectual abilities. It cannot be taken over as secondhand merchandise by someone else without considerable loss of value.

Too much living with the thoughts of others leads to stultification of one's own creative abilities, which are the highest manifestations of the human soul. The academic vice is erudition and classification instead of personal creation.

68

Altruism forms the basis of Christian civilization. "Love thy neighbor as thyself" and "Do unto others as you would have them do unto you" are different forms of the second of the two commandments that Jesus said were the foundation of his teaching. The first was "Thou shalt love the Lord thy God with all thy heart, and with all thy soul, and with all thy mind" (Matthew

22:37). However, unlike the Jews, Christians generally do not feel an intimate relationship with their God. The feeling of most Christians toward God is not one of love; it is more awe, respect, or fear, but not love. For love, one must feel close to the loved one. Christians do not have this feeling as do pious Jews. They may love Jesus or the Virgin Mary, but it is not quite the same as loving God the Almighty.

Consequently, altruism or investment in the well-being of others is the most important commandment for Christians. They may not always follow this commandment in their behavior, but the ideal is ever there. Christians everywhere make a point of trying to be generous, helpful, compassionate, and to the degree possible for them, loving toward those with whom they are in contact. They believe this represents following the will of God in their daily lives. *Egotism* and/or *narcissism* are two of the worst sins of which an individual can be accused. As an almost necessary result of this attitude, personal self-development does not occupy a high place in the Christian scheme of human virtues. Anyone who spends too much time or resources on his or her own self is looked upon with suspicion by Christians. Personal ambition is acceptable as long as there are generous, charitable dispensations connected to it. *Selfishness* is a crushing epithet leveled against anyone.

It is not surprising, therefore, that personal development, which is another way of referring to metaphysical development, is not a prominent feature of Christian civilization. A degree of selfishness is necessary in order to develop the soul. Personal development does not come easily since its goal is spiritualization, a difficult process. It requires continuous and intensive attention to self—'selfishness.'

* * *

Those who give themselves over to "helping" others often wind up as mental children themselves instead of as spiritual adults. This tendency is seen in members of the so-called "helping" professions like doctors, social workers, pastors, teachers, and all the other professions in which practitioners make their living "helping" others. The higher duty to self is usually neglected. Furthermore, it is important to remember that it is a very difficult thing to know what kind of help is in the real interest of others. Giving candy bars to a hungry person is not in their best interest. Much could be said about the ultimate undesirability of furnishing charity instead of opportunity to needy individuals. Habituation to charity, even the subtle type like "affirmative action," is one of the most unfortunate things that can happen to a person in need of self-development.

The first responsibility of a human being is to develop one's self. If one fails to meet this responsibility, his or her life will ultimately become a failure. The determination of how to fulfill this responsibility is the single most important problem of human life. In this sense, Christianity leads its adherents down a false path.

* * *

The nineteenth century German philosopher Max Stirner had much of interest to say about the above remarks in the one book that he published entitled *Der Einzige und sein Eigentum.* Translating the title has been the despair of translators; the generally accepted English version has been the incomprehensible "The Ego and its Own." I have ventured to provide my own translation, "The Unique Self and its Prerogatives." This title may have more meaning to anyone interested in exploring the thoughts of Stirner.

Max Stirner only gets footnotes now in textbooks of philosophy, largely because of his polemical and obtuse style of writing. Even beyond that, his basic idea about the significance of self has been subjected to withering criticisms at virtually all levels of society. I think, however, that his concept is of great importance and deserves much more attention by those interested in unconventional ideas, whether they are philosophers, ethicists, psychologists, or just those who wish to enlarge their consciousness of the human condition.

69

The other day I found it necessary to drive my aged vehicle to Tucson, about 75 miles from my cabin. Arriving in that city from my forest home is like leaving the Amazon jungle for Rio de Janeiro. It is drastically changing worlds. Everything is different and strange, a difficult experience for someone my age. Vehicles are the predominant presence, moving in every direction, and producing in me an almost panic reaction about driving in such milieu. Besides the vehicles, the city seems entirely composed of shops, service stations, and restaurants. Interspersed are rows and rows of houses although there seemed to be no people in their vicinity.

Finally, I managed to park at one of the great supershops to obtain the few items I needed. Entering it was like entering a maze of passageways with stuff of every type on either side of the narrow ways and people milling about seemingly aimlessly. I couldn't find what I wanted. Soon I became disoriented and felt I might fall. There was no place to sit down. One of the salespeople noticed my distress and helped me to the restrooms where there were a couple of uncomfortable iron chairs. After a time, I felt better and was able to make my way out of the facility without purchasing anything. It was a relief to drive home.

I don't know how people live under these conditions. For me today, it would be impossible. Many years ago, I lived in New York and Paris, two of the great metropolises of the world, but I don't remember experiencing in them this feeling of impersonal pressures combined with such a sense of human emptiness. More evidence that I am totally unsuited for life in twenty-first century America.

70

The dichotomy between the figures of Johann Wolfgang von Goethe (1749–1832) and Paul Gauguin (1848–1903) has always interested me. Both of these individuals represent human creativity at its highest level: Goethe in literature, Gauguin in painting. Yet they exhibited profound differences in the way that they related to their own societies. Goethe was the "successful" person *par excellence,* obtaining rewards and recognition during his lifetime. He was successful as a writer, as a public figure, and as an administrator, and even accomplished important work in science. He died at 83 years of age surrounded by admirers and honors. Goethe's long poetical masterpiece *Faust* is generally regarded as the greatest work of its genre of modern times.

On the other hand, Gauguin was the "unsuccessful" person *par excellence.* He was always at odds with society and wished to escape from it. He was chronically short of money and had great difficulty selling his paintings. He exiled himself to an isolated island in French Polynesia, living with a pubescent Tahitian girl. Gauguin died prematurely in miserable circumstances at 55 years of age. To this day, there is considerable uncertainty about his merits as an artist and his fame rests more on the exotic (and erotic) nature of his life than on admiration of his work. Little attention is paid to Gauguin's confessional prose work *Avant et Après.* When he asked August Strindberg, another great rebel, to write an introduction for one of his rare showings, the latter declined, saying he really did not understand Gauguin's painting.

Goethe was a man who knew how to cotton to society; Gauguin was exactly the opposite. He was an inveterate nay-sayer. What can be said about the relative *value* of these two highly intelligent and creative individuals? For most observers, there would be no contest. Goethe, who became the great icon of German literature, would seem to be a vastly superior person to Gauguin, who has been portrayed as an irresponsible escapist, a radical non-conformist, and a person who was antagonistic to his society and contributed nothing to it.

I have to admit that my own life much more closely resembles that of Gauguin than of Goethe. It is true that my financial circumstances are better than his were; however, I have not received the modicum of recognition that he did even when he was alive. I have followed the former's example, certainly not that of Goethe, never mind the fact that I do not have the literary talents of that poetical genius. But I do not feel defensive about the model I have chosen to follow. Gauguin to me represents a more *important* type of human being than Goethe. He was almost a Christ-like figure, willing to sacrifice himself for the sake of expressing what he thought and felt. Goethe was conciliatory (as he himself admitted in private conversation—a true politician!); he was willing to overlook his deeper insights for the sake of his harmonious adaptation to the world. For me, Goethe ultimately becomes boring like a Sunday sermon, while Gauguin is forever interesting and instructive. I believe that, in the long run, saying No! to society is more important than saying yes to it, more important than equivocating or, worst of all, saying nothing. The naysayers are the engines of spiritual progress—if progress there is to be. It is easy to just go along; it is hard to change course. But human society, like a ship on the high seas, must often change its course if it is to survive.

* * *

The metaphysical issues facing Gauguin have been acutely delineated in Somerset Maugham's novel *The Moon and the Sixpence.* Charles Strickland represents a thinly disguised Gauguin, isolated, working madly, and finally dying alone on a Pacific island. Maugham has no answers to the problem of Strickland—or of Gauguin—but he clearly poses the problems they faced, since he was a brilliant novelist and an honest thinker. The same issues are posed in a different manner by the character Larry in *The Razor's Edge.* I don't know of any English language novelist after Maugham who has been able to represent the motivational issues facing creative spirits with such insight and virtuosity. Thomas Mann might qualify with his *Doktor Faustus.* No writers I know of in today's world seem conscious of these issues.

* * *

Philosophers should have the high responsibility of awakening creative minds to the metaphysical issues of human life—instead of leaving it to novelists. But unfortunately it is a responsibility that they have abandoned for many years. One may hope that some day they will reassume their task.

71

I am only interested in *existential* literature that reflects the total existence of an individual. Mere intellectual wordiness does not touch me any longer. Thus I have preferred the sayings of Antisthenes to the discourses of Plato, the life of Diogenes of Sinope to the logical essays of Aristotle, the writings of Augustine to those of Aquinas, Kierkegaard and Nietzsche to Kant or Hegel. In modern times, Berdyaev and Shestov are shining beacons to me compared to Heidegger or Husserl. Regarding contemporary philosophy professors of the "analytic" persuasion, I do not consider them independent philosophers, but rather as members of an academic guild.

Rationalizing philosophy is meaningless if it does not arise from the soul and way of life of the philosopher. The philosophers of today are inferior to those of antiquity or even to the medieval scholastics because they are lacking the key ingredient of a philosopher—a total commitment to one's philosophy. Today, philosophy is enchained in a scholarly prison called academia devoid of spiritual significance. Academics avoid the term "soul" because they do not believe in its existence; it indicates a backward mentality to them, appropriate perhaps for literary writings but not for scholarly pursuits. But those who are not conscious of their own souls and not devoted to its well-being cannot produce meaningful philosophy.

Genuine philosophers are of no value to the material elements of society nor do they provide entertainment to the public. Already Seneca noted in his *Epistles* that the Roman populace preferred the gladiatorial cruelties to the lectures of philosophers. The only possible benefit of philosophy to people is in revealing the metaphysical depths of human life. This they do not do through didactic teaching but through demonstrating with their lives and minds a higher form of existence. Diogenes of Sinope, an antique philosopher scorned by academia except for historical purposes, asked what good is a philosopher who spends all his time philosophizing but does not disturb anyone. Who is disturbed by the philosophers of today, pontificating with incomprehensible jargons in their ivory towers?

72

Every philosopher sooner or later desires to produce a *System* reflecting his realities and I am no exception to that rule. But it is important to recognize that creation of this "System" is entirely a function of the psychological need of a philosopher. He needs to create his vision of the world in an organized form in order to be comfortable with himself. No one else pays attention to philosophers' systems except for college students of philosophy or the occasional academic who analyzes them for professional reasons. Who cares about the systems of Spinoza, Schopenhauer, Hegel, Royce, or Whitehead—never mind the countless ones produced by lesser figures? No one does in my estimation. However, that does not detract from the *deep personal need* of a philosopher to objectify his view of the world. Why does he have this need? I am not prepared to say or even speculate. But I shall outline mine anyway, in spite of not knowing why I do. My system is a tripartite one; it is based on the realms of physical sciences, of life sciences, and of spirituality. One needs to distinguish among these three realms that exist on different levels of reality:

Physical science—This is the reality of material substance or, more accurately, of energy since, as I have discussed above, there is much evidence that the core of "hard" matter is fundamentally packets of energy. Here is where natural law applies: the laws of gravitation, thermodynamics, and electromagnetism.

Science has revealed the immensity of the physical cosmos and the complex energetics of apparently simple matter. For many people, material substance *is* reality; everything else is transient superstructure or window dressing. For them, the *force* of operative physical energy is the reality underlying everything. There is no doubt that material reality is something ever present and must be always considered as a factor to be dealt with in conceptions of the universe.

Life science—In spite of all the advances of physical science, the phenomenon of life is still a mystery to it. All the studies of DNA and brain electricity only describe life; they do not explain its appearance, maintenance, or disappearance. The *Élan Vital* (the concept of Henri Bergson) is still the most appropriate term for describing the life force. Life, from primitive protoplasm to elaborate human social or herd groupings, is something that is superimposed upon the inanimate matter of physical science. A will to survival and propagation is its principal feature. I believe to think of life as some biochemical entity emerging from a primeval ooze, a chance material event occurring over millions of years, is to miss its true metaphysical nature. A Ptolemaic view of the universe with planet Earth at the center is still relevant when considering the significance of life. So far, there is no reason to believe life or anything analogous to it exists anywhere else. If this should change, my views would have to change.

Spirituality—As life is added on to inanimate matter, so spirit appears to be "superimposed" upon life. Inexplicably, the phenomenon of spirituality emerges out of life. The first and most important new feature is that the living being acquires consciousness, albeit fluctuating in intensity and of self, of knowledge, of values, or even of an ultimate Divinity. No such consciousness is connected to simple life as is witnessed by nature, "red in fang and claw." The term "soul" refers to the intensification of spirit in individuals, principally human beings, but perhaps higher mammals to a degree. Spirit has only relevance for the individual self; it is nonexistent in groupings or herds. There is no such thing as "the spirit of the times" or a "nationalistic spirit"; these are always imaginary abstractions conceived by thinkers entranced by sociology. In the human condition, spirit is a metaphysical reality for *individuals*; thus concepts based on physics, biology, or especially sociological classifications are not applicable to it.

Spirit is free, spirit is transcendental; therefore, it extends beyond the limits and constraints of sensory experience. Not all human beings realize their spirituality; those who do not are no more capable of being aware of spirituality than is a blind person capable of being aware of color. However, one can become spiritual through a process of self-discovery. Human beings yearn toward spirituality just as animals yearn to live; this is a special quality of the species *Homo sapiens.* They realize dimly that behind the *phenomenal* world of living, there must be a *transcendental* reality that has initiated and is involved with the former. This realization is a constant in human history, starting with primitive animism up to the most sophisticated concepts of an ultimate deity. No more than life can exist in our solar system without the heat-giving reality of the sun, so spiritual entities could not exist without a spirit-giving reality traditionally called "God." I cannot imagine otherwise about my soul.

But just because one cannot imagine something does not mean that it may not be true. Whether or not there is truly an underlying metaphysical groundwork, a spiritual Divinity, a "God" in the sense of a greater spiritual reality removed from oneself, is a question for every individual human being to ponder on himself. I have not directly experienced such a God; so for me, He is only an "epistemological necessity," meaning that I cannot think of my own spirituality except as occurring in relation to some greater metaphysical reality. I have felt that upon death my spirit might rejoin the greater one and contribute to its greatness. That is all the immortality I would like to have. One might regard this concept as the ultimate justification for individual spiritual development. But it arises from no revelation or even intuition; I have to admit it is a hopeful human idea with all the uncertainties connected to merely human ideas. However, it has a *pragmatic value* and, according to William James whose opinions I greatly respect, believing it may help bring it into the domain of reality.

* * *

This is my smaller "system" of thought about reality that is already a bit too long with its digressions on spirit and deity. It is not to be compared with the imposing systems encompassing large tomes elaborated by famous philosophers. But it is suitable for me, a forest philosopher, who is far removed from the congresses, conferences, meetings, seminars, and publications of the world of scholarship and technical philosophy.

73

I am struck by the prevalence of use of names of great philosophers and thinkers by academics who capitalize on them to form societies, clubs, circles, or associations in which the academics are important officials. Doubtless, some good is obtained by maintaining the memory of these philosophers. And, doubtless, being officers in these societies fills out curriculum vitae and helps the individuals concerned to obtain academic advancement. Still I cannot get used to the names of Thoreau or Nietzsche being used for self-serving purposes when these organizations stand for everything these great men opposed. Thoreau would have never been a member of a Thoreau Society; Nietzsche made it clear he wanted no followers. But that has not deterred ambitious individuals from using their names and reputations.

Although obscurity should protect me, the wrath of my spirit would fall upon anyone who might use my name for such purposes. The name Leon Landesman is sacred and not to be touched by profane hands. Of course, Nietzsche said essentially the same and much good it did him. Now Nietzsche societies proliferate everywhere like wild weeds in a unique garden.

74

Lately I have noticed an increase in drone activity in the skies overhead. Drones are supposed to fly too high to be audible on the ground but that seems not to be the case here. They emit a low "droning" sound that is often irritating to me. It reminds me of the country in which I live in case I should be inclined to forget. There is a drone training base in nearby Sierra Vista but it is more likely that these drones are on the hunt for illegal crossers. These poor devils are taking great risks to find something that I have categorically rejected. The new life that represents shining success for them would be a miserable failure for me. We are all members of the same species *Homo sapiens* so the question arises as to why our aspirations and attitudes are so different?

An obvious answer is that the affluent society in which I grew up provided education and opportunities that were denied to them and left them at the mercy of an impoverished milieu. Yet while lack of education and opportunity may explain the *illegales'* precarious lives and willingness to risk all for a better environment, their availability does not explain the outcome of my life. None of my former confreres (to my knowledge) have taken my route; all have made their adaptations to society. Utilizing Darwinian terminology, I am a natural variation that has no survival value. I must be a "sport" due to a chance mutation that cannot propagate itself biologically, societally, or intellectually.

This depressing thought creeps up on me when I allow myself to lapse into the conventional thinking of the world around me. But there is an alternative hypothesis that I prefer. From a metaphysical perspective, it may be enough that only one of me should have existed. It may not be necessary in the cosmic order of reality for my type to be repeated. There may be no need for more than one soul like mine. This to me is a more satisfying concept, which from the point of view of philosophical pragmatism acts to strengthen my psychological existence.

75

My name in the Yiddish language is a misnomer. There are no other individuals I can call "*landsman,*" meaning countryman. (I don't know a suitable English equivalent; "countryman" is too weak.) I am the sole resident of my spiritual country. When I pass on, it will no longer exist. *Sic transit Gloria mundi* refers not only to the transitory nature of fame, but also to the brief nature of individual human existence. What remains behind is just a husk, a weak materialization of one's spiritual nature. Yet a developed soul may have enriched a greater metaphysical reality. This is an audacious thought but one that provides a metaphysically intelligible explanation for the remarkable spiritual development occurring in human beings. It provides a pragmatic *teleology* that makes sense for understanding the appearance of spirit in human beings.

The development of souls can be thought of as analogous to glaciers melting in the Arctic that produce rising waters inundating all the low-lying areas of the globe. Like a melting glacier's effect on the material world, the emergence of a soul can affect the entire metaphysical universe. The consequences of this event are quite unpredictable, as Emerson eloquently described in his essay *Circles.*

If God has a separate existence, I don't think He wants sacrifices, prayers, rituals, obedience, or even a self-serving love. He must want humans to be *conscious* of the transcendental nature of their existence and therefore available in their relationship to him. This only comes from human living—in the widest sense of the term. Without a transcendental consciousness, Emersonian self-reliance becomes narcissistic egocentricity. Those who have not acquired this consciousness should stick to religions that can serve as ersatz substitutes for it.

76

It is natural for youth to be mad for things, for people, and for travel adventures. Their focus is appropriately external, centered on their surroundings. But with maturity, as things of the world are put in perspective, a *transcendental consciousness* develops in the mind of a human being. One comes to realize that there is more to human life than what enters it through the senses. He or she should become aware of their soul and of spiritual realities. It is sad, even repulsive, to see a person of mature age who still exhibits the attitudes and interests of youth. It means that his life has been stunted; it has failed to develop in the manner for which it was meant. This mental stunting is promoted by a society in its emphasis on values that are appropriate for the young but not for mature individuals.

77

The justification of "philosophy" is the philosopher himself. Everything he says and writes enlarges and deepens his own mind. What is present on paper as his writing is only the symbol of the reality that has formed within him—more precisely within his soul. The writing is the objectivized symbol of what the thinker has become. When others read his writing, they gain only a dim grasp of the realities within him. That is why philosophers try constantly to improve the linguistic representation of their ideas. Ultimately, it is usually better to think out one's own views of self and the world rather than to rely on representations of others.

All the vast quantity of philosophic tomes bears a similar relationship to their authors as do statues of famous men to the men themselves. They are only more or less superficial images of the realities of the individuals whose mental or physical status they depict. For obscure reasons, Plato decided that metaphysical Ideas (as revealed by his own philosophical writings) counted for everything and real individuals for very little. Perhaps the chaos in Greek society during his lifetime had something to do with his attitude. In late Old Testament Hebrew scriptures, the concept of "Wisdom" plays a very similar role. Through a quirk of intellectual history, Plato's impact on the Catholic Church became enormous except that an Almighty God took the place of the Ideas. The development of humanism and pragmatism in contemporary philosophy began to rectify these imaginary worldviews but has been successful to only a limited degree.

Besides the Church, Plato is a great icon of Western academic philosophy since he put "philosophy" as an abstraction on a pedestal of supremacy. In an oft-quoted statement, Alfred North Whitehead wrote that all Western philosophy is a footnote to Plato. This attitude fits in very well with the departmental structure of Western universities. How else could philosophy with all its vagaries over the years have survived as a unitary abstract concept? It would have long since gone the way of astrology, alchemy, and magic.

Instead of studying philosophy, great minds like Augustine, Spinoza, Emerson, and Nietzsche should be studied and experienced as the individuals they were and not as producers of philosophy. There are instructional treatises on philosophy and metaphysics that one can read without ever coming across the name of an individual thinker! Philosophy would be far more pertinent to the human condition if the emphasis were placed on individuals and not on an obsolete abstraction. The term "philosophy" itself in the antique Greek means "love of wisdom." How far removed from that definition is what passes for university philosophy today. There is no wisdom without wise men.

78

Formerly I wrote out my historical autobiography, but now I wish to concentrate on my spiritual one. When I was a youth, I was quite spiritually minded. My interests were focused upon the spiritual realities behind the material appearances. I had only a vague idea what these might be but I felt there must be something more to my life than the constant getting and spending that went on all around me. Since I grew up in a nonreligious home and religion was held in low repute by most of my peers, I had to satisfy my spiritual yearnings by some other means. I discovered *philosophy.* It seemed to me to offer the kind of spiritual satisfactions that I yearned to obtain. (I use the term *spiritual* in its broadest meaning, not in the restricted Christian sense of pious effusions.) At first, I devoured the classical philosophers—Plato, the Stoics, Epicurus, Marcus Aurelius, and others. Then I discovered Spinoza, Schopenhauer, Emerson, Thoreau, and Nietzsche—especially Nietzsche. These thinkers opened up whole new worlds to me, far beyond the banalities of my daily life. For some inexplicable reason, it did not occur to me that all the philosophers in which I was interested lived centuries, even millennia, ago.

Since I was not content to be a mere reader of philosophy, I began to think how I myself could become a philosopher. War interrupted my ability to pursue this path but it certainly intensified my interest in it. Finally, I reached a point where I had to decide what to do with my life. It was clear to me that the only place where philosophers existed at the present time was in seminaries or universities. The days of the independent philosophers of the antique world were long over. During the Christian era of Europe, philosophy had been incorporated into religious institutions; now it had moved into the universities. Outside of seminaries and universities, there was no place for philosophers. Apart from these, philosophy was not taken seriously.

Since I was an unsuitable candidate for the seminary, I did what was necessary to enter academic life. I obtained my doctoral degree and published my dissertation. But it did not take long for me to realize that what I understood as philosophy did not exist in universities. Philosophy there consisted of "impartial" analytic approaches to everything I deemed worthy of reverence. Cognitive and linguistic sciences were thought to be the substance of philosophy. The objectivity of the scientific mindset reigned supreme. The "philosophers" who were my colleagues followed Husserl's dictum that philosophy must be strict science. I found metaphysics to be nonexistent in American universities except as a subject of historical interest. What had attracted me to philosophy had no credibility in academic life. The reaction of Socrates upon reading Anaxagoras' book (as recounted in the *Phaedo*) duplicated my experience exactly. I was a duck out of water with my spiritual interests and an uncomfortable isolate in the world of American "philosophy."

At that time, I was subject to constant anxieties since I dearly wanted to be accepted by my confreres and achieve success in academic life. This was not to be. However, I now realize that my time in academia was beneficial for me. I learned to become intellectually self-reliant and not depend on approval of my peers—the latter a requirement that is essential for survival as an independent philosopher. I developed my own *Weltanschauung*, something I feel to be the principal need for personal success of an individual. I left academia and became *my own person* in all aspects of my life.

What I have learned to value above all else is my own soul. Very few people today really understand or even believe in the existence of their souls. In my former life in the university if I had expressed belief in a metaphysical soul, I would have been laughed out of court and dismissed as an eccentric. Consequently, I have relied on my own judgments in this matter. When I came across Nietzsche's assertion that "the noble soul has reverence for itself" (*Beyond Good and Evil*), I experienced a great rush of gratitude for finally I had found someone who felt as I did and was not afraid to say so. Admittedly, Nietzsche paid a heavy price for his boldness—a price I am not prepared to pay.

The intellectual foundation for belief in the soul has been recently set forth by Richard Schain in an essay entitled *Souls Exist*. I do not feel the necessity for such an elaborate defense of my belief. I *know* that my soul exists in a way that I know nothing else. If this belief is unfounded, then my whole life has been a serious error. But I do not think my life has been an error. I think that those who do not attend to their own souls are the ones who have made the error.

Immanuel Kant in his famous treatise *Critique of Pure Reason* demolished metaphysics in secular philosophy and gave it over entirely to faith-based religion. I have often wondered if I could find what I want in one of the contemporary religions.

But I did not develop in an atmosphere of belief in the Judeo-Christian God and cannot now see it as more than a phase in one's mental development analogous to flat earth conviction or the Ptolemaic belief in planet Earth as the center of the universe. The fact is the idea of God does not have the *immediacy* for me the way that belief in my soul does. It is not possible to truly participate in any of the monotheisms without faith in an almighty, all-knowing, providential God. This kind of faith I do not have nor do I want.

79

Unamuno's Prophecy. The Italian writer Giovanni Papini published a satirical work in 1951 entitled *Il Libro Nero* (The Black Book). It is little known to English readers since it has not been translated into their idiom. In it, Papini attributes to the philosopher Miguel de Unamumo fragments of a play entitled "The First and the Last." The first is the man Adam developed by God to be a superior creature with a body and a soul. The last is the last person living on Earth before the cataclysmic destruction of the planet. The latter has only a number (W. S. 347926), not a name, since names had been long abandoned by human society. He is a mechanical being that resembles a machine, having been formed by scientific methods. He has no soul. He is entirely a product of the mechanical world in which he exists. Somehow the two creatures meet just before the end of the world, but they have nothing to say to one another since they have nothing in common. Adam had been created by Jehovah, while W. S. 347926 was constructed by Hanuman, the Monkey God of Hindu theology. The fragment ends with a long discourse by W. S. 347926 disclaiming any connection to Adam (or Adam's God) and stating that Hanuman was his true progenitor.

Of course it is all tongue in cheek as was Papini's habit. He included in the book a similarly unflattering vignette about Picasso that was so realistic that Picasso forced him to publically state it was a fictional portrayal. There is always a point, however, to Papini's satires as is the case with every satirist. "The First and the Last" is a grim picture of the direction he saw humanity to be taking. The direction is toward a mechanized, soulless, automaton-like existence, as if it were the product of a demonic monkey god. He has not been alone in this vision.

* * *

Why is Friedrich Nietzsche so popular today among those who have an interest in the important issues of their lives? One has only to examine the number of books by or about Nietzsche on philosophy bookshelves of general bookstores to confirm his popularity. Yet much of his writing is difficult to read and often contradictory. Few readers understand his subtle allusions to historical figures in philosophy and religion. His life hardly inspires confidence in his wisdom or prophetic abilities. So why is he so popular?

I maintain it is because he is the greatest *naysayer* in the history of philosophy and our society is yearning for naysayers. There is a dim awareness among people that they are on the wrong track in the structure of their lives. Nietzsche represents someone who has the knowledge, insight, and capability to say nay to what is happening in Western civilization. That is why he is so popular among thoughtful individuals today.

80

Every serious person at some time or another faces the question, "Is there any purpose to my life?" It is a question that has often recurred in my mind. The question can be easily extended beyond the individual; is there any purpose to human life in general, to the overall phenomenon of life, even to the universe as a whole? Why anything at all—or is everything just a chance throw of the dice? Of course there is no definitive answer to any of these questions, but it is worthwhile for an individual to consider them and to try to relate them to his own existence.

In the case of human life, while its purpose seems beyond human ken, a related question may be more answerable—namely, has there been any "progress" achieved by humanity? At first glance, when one compares the caveman to the humans of modernity, the question seems absurd—of course there has been progress, enormous progress. The fact that I sit here writing a spiritual journal in comfort, without fear or hunger, illustrates the progress that has been made. Yet one must consider that progress may not be a constant. It may not follow a continuous upward slope; it may exhibit a bell-shaped curve in which at a certain point upward progression is supplanted by downward retrogression.

There is much reason to believe that the human species is retrogressing at the present time. The only progress now is technological in nature, which cannot be equated with human progress. Through the primacy of technology, natural forces have been overcome but the essential feature of the human condition, the human soul, has been diminished. Wars and terrorism have worsened in their impact on society and development of an individual's soul has given way to an emphasis on soulless technology. The human species is spreading over the face of the planet like an uncontrollable fungus and is threatening to make life unsustainable earlier than anyone might have imagined. More and more, the psychology described by Boccaccio in survivors of the medieval bubonic plague. "Eat, drink, and be merry" (*The Decameron)* seems to describe the contemporary denizens of planet Earth. Perhaps even more appropriate was the remark of Louis XV just prior to the convulsions of the French Revolution,

"*Après moi, le déluge.*"

With this sense of impending doom of the species, the only rational "eschatological" attitude is to consider the purpose of one's own particular life. Even if one dutifully pays his dues to society, there may be only a few generations to come in the future. While consideration of the purpose of one's own life may be quite obscure, certain possibilities nay, even probabilities, can be ascertained. This discovery should be the responsibility of philosophers, which is why Plato considered them to be the rightful leaders of society. Epicurus, who was one of the most unmetaphysical of the philosophers of antiquity, stated that one was never too old or too young to immerse himself in philosophy. However, the recognition of the importance of philosophy that appeared during antiquity has vanished—a significant sign of retrogression of the human species.

When the universe and its contents as a whole are considered, it is self-evident that everything must come to its appointed end. Solar systems come and go; our own sun must burn itself up some day and with it, the end of life on Earth. Many of the species of life that have emerged on the earth have already disappeared, leaving only faint traces for the employment of paleontologists. There is no reason to believe that the same will not happen to Homo sapiens, one of the most fragile of mammalian species. Many relatively advanced societies have disappeared. As far as individual life is concerned, every one of us must disappear or pass over one day, as the case may be.

It is essential to recognize that disappearance from terrestrial existence does not necessarily mean the entire disappearance of a human being. The survivors of someone's death know nothing of the fate of his soul since the souls of defunct individuals do not (apparently) communicate with them. However, this failure of communication does not prove nonexistence. The fact that the physical body is in the grave is no more proof of the soul's nonexistence than the empty pot from which water has boiled out proves nonexistence of molecules of H_20. They still exist but in a different form, not visible to the human eye. Of course, if one is blind to the existence of a soul distinguishable from the physical self, this line of reasoning is meaningless.

Consider again the nature of the human soul. It may have striven throughout its terrestrial life for consciousness of the world within which it found itself. It may have striven for consciousness of its own nature. It may have exhibited the quality of creativity in ways unique to itself, from creating works of art to acquiring fortunes. At the least, it may have striven to survive in a hostile environment. For these purposes, it has had to maintain its freedom from the tyranny of nature and, to a degree, from society itself. In these manifold ways, it has striven to develop itself beyond a basic level. One may ask why has it striven so much to surpass itself?

It is reasonable, if not compelling, to perceive a transcendental purpose revealing itself in the soul's activity. The greatest thinkers of the world from Aristotle to Einstein have perceived a "divine" purpose acting in the universe, although concepts of divinity have varied greatly. The purpose of the human soul, in exhibiting its resemblance to a purposeful divinity, does not require its immortality. It may make its contribution to divinity in a way that is far removed from our limited perceptive abilities—perhaps serving as spiritual alimentation for a dynamic, still-developing deity. This to me is a more reasonable concept than evaporation into nothingness after a lifetime of development. Such a concept need not apply to all souls; only the ones that have proven themselves worthy may be suitable as alimentation for divinity.

Those "empirical materialists" who refuse to recognize the spirituality of the human condition are like tourists who only notice the architectural monuments of the lands they visit. They do not learn about the ethos, the culture, the way of life, or the spiritual history of the people who inhabit the land. Thus, they miss out on their essential features and might as well have stayed at home. A similar but more tragic fate awaits the materialists who are not conscious of the human soul. They might as well never have been born.

81

Generally I have a poor memory for events that have happened to me in the past. Names of people or things are especially hard for me to recall. However, there are certain events that I vividly remember as though they occurred yesterday, even though they may date from forty, fifty, even sixty years ago. These are the *erotic experiences* that I have had in my life. It is as if they have been permanently imprinted in my memory. The only events comparable to them are some of my war experiences, which are also vivid memories for me.

By erotic experiences, I don't mean mere phallic penetration and orgasm epitomized by the cowboy expression, "slam, bam, thank you ma'am!" Nor do I refer to the romantic poetry of the medieval troubadours or poets like Dante and Petrarch whose "erotic" love dispensed with its bodily aspect. I regard erotic experiences as the merging of two bodies and two souls that is unique within the human condition. A quote is appropriate from Schain's essay "The Meaning of the Erotic Impulse" (*Philosophical Artwork,* 1983):

> The power of authentic erotic expression lies in its spiritual nature in an increasingly spiritless world. In no other human activity does man's body and spirit act in such harmony. When a person is joined to his lover, he leaves mundane daily life and

> receives an intimation of the meaning of escape from time and space. Lost in the depths of erotic feelings, he undergoes an experience like none other in this vale of tears. Restlessness and striving fly away through the miracle of erotic fulfillment [italics L.L.]. For once, he is at peace with himself.

* * *

Some may think this is just sentimental romanticizing. They are probably the ones who have never experienced erotic fulfillment.

82

How is one to acquire a sense of the significance of his spiritual self if he feels he is merely a momentary event in the vastness of the material universe? There must be a change in perspective from self as brief event to self as a creative force, from reactively living one's life to deliberately creating one's soul. Only then does a person become *homo spiritualis*, a center of a spiritual universe whose significance cannot be assessed by him.

83

Forming a conception of an ultimate metaphysical reality is obviously impossible for ordinary human beings. It is no more possible than for a human mind to form a conception of distances involved in billions of light years. Rather than dwell on this impossibility, it is better to think about the attraction it exerts on our own souls. The evidence of this attraction is the ever-present tendency toward *religiosity*, which is a sense of the transcendental, of holiness, and ineffability. Another way of expressing this tendency is to label it as the *metaphysical need* of mankind.

Human nature being what it is, religious institutions tend toward decay the longer they remain a force in human affairs. This is true of all institutions but is particularly noticeable in religious ones. The psychological power of tradition tends to perpetuate religions as can be seen in the major religions of the world. But religion is not synonymous with the religiosity of individuals. The deterioration of religious institutions does not do away with their metaphysical need. Every thoughtful person ought to find a way of satisfying his metaphysical need independently of superannuated religions.

What do I mean by superannuated religions? I mean the replacement of genuine religiosity (spirituality) by institutionalized material structures that have nothing to do with the human spirit. In Judaism, tradition and ritualism long ago became more important than religiosity; in Roman Catholicism, hierarchical structures inherited from a defunct Roman empire have done the same; in Protestant Christianity, the fetish of a Holy Bible and an imaginary companion named Jesus drown out spiritual creativity of individuals. All these tendencies are profoundly anti-spiritual and need to be opposed by genuinely religious individuals.

There is no substitute for a person developing his own religious conceptions and expressions. He can enrich his own spirituality through experiences, through learning, and through contact with other spiritual individuals; but all those must be supportive, not prescriptive, of his own metaphysical consciousness. An article of faith that has emerged in my mind is that my own spiritual development contributes to the ultimate metaphysical reality called God. I can't say how I have come to this belief. Some may label it a delusion or a blasphemous illusion and so it must seem to those who do not share this feeling. I have no desire to persuade anyone of its reality. However, sometime, in some way or another, I believe this truth will out for every deep-thinking person.

84

It is my opinion that the origins of Christian anti-Semitism can be found in the feelings of Christians that by rejecting the divinity of Jesus Christ, the Jews rejected the spiritual values of Christianity. Thus they were looked upon as a corrupted people, impervious to the new spiritual insights of the new religion and potentially undermining of them. The notorious clannishness of Jews contributed to this attitude. It may be a long way from Christian judgment about their parental Judaism to the *autos-da-fé* of the Inquisition or to the colder murders of the Nazi gas chambers, but I believe the connection exists.

* * *

Girolamo Savonarola who lived and preached in Renaissance Florence was a Christ-like figure. Great similarities exist between his life and that of Jesus Christ. However, the interrogation of Jesus was more humane than that of Savonarola and history has treated the former in a far kinder manner.

* * *

St. Anthony in the thirteenth century: "Happy is the man through whom the Holy Spirit speaks and not his own self." A more appropriate statement for today is: "Happy is the man who speaks out of his own spirit and not his societal self."

* * *

Writing strengthens my soul. Reading diverts it into often unworthy pathways. Schopenhauer wrote that reading is thinking with another person's brain, certainly an undesirable state of affairs. Reading for me may be suitable for casual entertainment (example: reading Agatha Christie or Sherlock Holmes mysteries) but not for the serious business of my existence. But on certain occasions I gain something personally meaningful by reading. These are very special events in my life, which I embed in my memory and bring back again and again into my consciousness.

85

It is not enough for me to maintain my self as it is. Something within drives me to extend it in new dimensions of being. Having exhausted all means of developing myself through the physical world, I have turned to the metaphysical one. This is a more promising frontier for me. However, movement from the physical plane of reality to the metaphysical plane is a difficult process. The usual methods of assessing reality are of no value. A great deal of energy is needed to function on a metaphysical plane, especially in an age of scientism that denies metaphysical reality and only values material being. But metaphysical fulfillment is worth the effort because *Homo sapiens* is primarily a metaphysical creature.

I have discovered that movement to the metaphysical plane quickly involves an individual self with the ultimate metaphysical reality, a.k.a. God. This movement can be symbolized by $S < G$ (not $S = G$ as Vedanta teaches). The equation is also reversible, $G < S$, meaning that God verges into the self as well. The movement to the metaphysical plane is called *mysticism* and has a bad reputation due to the contemporary commitment of intellectuals to scientism. Mysticism is only acceptable today within the framework of traditional religious dogmas as part of the *modus vivendi* established between science and religion. However, mysticism needs to shake loose from the constraints of ancient religions and allow the metaphysical genius of individuals to come forth. Metaphysical fulfillment should not be dependent on a few apotheosized religious figures.

William James, when trying to define his philosophical theory of *Pragmatism* said, "truth is what works." He deferred elaborating on the meaning of "works." In my mind, what only truly works is the conscious self ascending from the physical to the metaphysical plane of existence. This I believe is the basic idea of Platonism. This ascent is *ineffable,* meaning it is beyond the power of language to describe. Language can only provide symbolic forms referring to the reality. Ludwig Wittgenstein in his famed *Tractatus Logico-Philosophicus* finally advocated abandoning language altogether and lapsing into silence. But a mysterious psychic force seems to drive individuals (like myself) to constantly create new linguistic symbols. These, however, should never be mistaken for metaphysical reality.

The well-known metaphysical need of people has to do with the movement of self onto a metaphysical plane of reality. When Christ asserted, "I and my Father are one," he revealed his discovery of a metaphysical plane of his existence (S < G). For some unworthy reason, the leaders of the religion that bears his name have denied this discovery to anyone else.

"Popery" is a nasty expression indicating rejection of the Roman Catholic system of rituals, authoritarianism, church wealth accumulation, and the like as having nothing to do with human spirituality. But all the religious symbols of today have become similarly corrupted. Popes, cathedrals, mosques, holy bibles, *mitzvahs*, Meccas—out with all of them! They corrupt the meaning of genuine spiritual states. They belong in the domain of education and history rather than in the religion of enlightened individuals.

86

I would replace use of the Sanskrit "Om" of Hinduism with the Aramaic "Abba" (father) found in St. Mark to convey metaphysical awareness. The latter conveys a sense of personalism that the Hindu expression lacks. If metaphysics is not personal—including the ultimate reality as well as the individual person, then it is useless to the human condition. The original sin of the offspring of Judaism was the urge to *universalize* their new religion, thus tending to depersonalize it. Orthodox Jewry has not fallen into this grievous error and thereby has maintained its intimate relationship with God. My own thoughts and writings are strictly directed toward Divinity and God alone will decide their fate.

To say that my thoughts and writings are for Divinity alone is not such a strange idea. Since time immemorial, people have given offerings to an Ultimate Reality in the form of their valuables, their animals, and even other humans. Even their children have been offered as sacrifices to God (Genesis 22). Although human sacrifice has been abandoned, the sacrifice of wealth to God has usually been encouraged by clerics who benefit greatly from this practice.

According to Christian scriptures, Jesus followed the tradition of the great Jewish prophets in minimizing the significance of sacrificing material valuables to God. He emphasized the importance of spiritual offerings. My writings are the most spiritual thing I can offer to Divinity. Even if I can't fully apprehend the nature of the ultimate spiritual reality, I can pay tribute to it in the form of my writings. This is why I want nothing to do with markets, fame, or societal recognition for these writings.

This would constitute sacrilegious behavior.

* * *

The Buddha was misinformed when he recurrently returned to the world for the benefit of mankind. He had had his day and should have left it at that. Jesus was more intelligent when he returned for only a brief stay and has since remained in the great beyond.

87

As far as fishing with one's writings in the public pond is concerned, Nietzsche was right: "There are no fish" for noble souls. The sooner one accepts this reality, the better off he will be. There never were any fish for Nietzsche, only posthumous blind worshipers, academics taking advantage of his notoriety, and the ignorant *Pöbel* always ready to follow popularity.

The many vicissitudes of the writer have been cataloged by Giovanni Papini in his book of essays entitled *The Devil Told Me.* However, he overlooked the main significance of serious writing, which is that by writing, the writer is simultaneously forming his soul. The writing itself is only the objective symbol of what has occurred in the writer's soul. If the writing is noble, the soul will have been formed in a similar manner. If it is hypocritical, banal, or aimed only at popularity, his soul will have been deformed.

* * *

The two principles underlying the human condition:

Honor your soul above all else.
Honor your soul's relationship with God.

Existential philosophy is the elaboration of these two principles.

* * *

Artists paint pictures, musicians play music, poets write poetry; I, being a philosopher, write what I feel and what I think.

88

Underlying the phenomena of daily life, there is a transcendental reality that initiates and sustains the former. Recognition of the importance of this insight motivated the transcendentalist movement of New England in the first half of the nineteenth century. Unfortunately for America, the transcendentalist writings have been relegated to the status of pastoral effusions, benign but meaningless. Just as no more than terrestrial energy can exist on the planet without a solar source, so metaphysical energy cannot exist without the transcendental source called God. One can hardly conceive otherwise. This conception has become a psychological necessity for me.

89

According to a Platonic myth, erotic love stems from the desire to merge with one's missing part. In my case, the missing part is an idealized female form. In past years, this desire has been a powerful passion in me and has been greatly responsible for the dissolution of my marriages. In my opinion, the erotic passion is *transcendental* in nature, meaning its nature is not explicable through mere forms of sensory perception. I see it as an additional form of Kant's transcendental aesthetic, except it is not a perception but a passion. The idea that it has anything to do with procreation seems utterly absurd to me since many individuals have always gone to great lengths to avoid procreating. The Roman Catholic doctrine that sexual intercourse is only justified for the sake of procreation reveals to me the metaphysical poverty of Catholic thought dealing with erotic love.

Erotic passion in me has not diminished with age although my genital functions have virtually disappeared. Eros is now a purer phenomenon in me since it is not contaminated by a procreative overlay. There are many more pleasurable avenues for merging with another than simple phallic penetration. But since I am now an old man, idealized female forms are rarely interested in me, which has probably saved me from much trouble. My erotic life is now largely confined to my dream world.

However, I have now discovered that a female form is not the only object with which I desire to merge. The desire to *physically* merge with an idealized female form is being replaced by a desire to *metaphysically* merge with the ultimate metaphysical reality—namely, God. I believe both of these desires originate from a similar source within me—perhaps deriving from Jacob Boehme's *Ungrund,* which he conceived of as the basic *desiring* groundwork of being, responsible for everything that is, even for Deity.

Many may feel that the erotic passion and the passion for God are not comparable phenomena. In the depths of my sensibility, I feel one leads into the other. One may admit that the desire to merge with the ultimate metaphysical reality represents a higher form of existential activity than do erotic impulses. But my experiences lead me to believe that they stem from the same transcendental passion and thus are comparable. To return to Plato, he was on a similar track when somewhere he asserts that recognition of *beauty* was en route to recognition of God. Dostoevsky went even further when he wrote that beauty would save the world (*The Idiot*).

The Renaissance writer Petrarch enunciated more forcefully than anyone the relationship between erotic passion and love of divinity. In his prose writing *My Secret* (written in Latin), Petrarch argues with his own alter ego, whom he arbitrarily named St. Augustine. Augustine points out that Petrarch's passion for Laura expressed in his *Canzoniere*, one of the great milestones of European poetical literature, has replaced his relationship with God. It becomes clear in the course of the discussion that the two relationships are intimately connected. Petrarch is reluctant to abandon his infatuation with Laura, but the reader senses that he is on the verge of replacing Laura with God as the recipient of his attentions.

In my mind, the connection between eros and spirituality is quite clear. I have only been attracted to women with both sexual and spiritual qualities. Plato was right in thinking that physical beauty was a stepping-stone to God. But the step is a steep one, and not easily ascended. Most do not take it.

The ideas expressed above could be developed further, especially in the area of physical merging, but since this writing is a journal and not a manual, I will refrain from the temptation.

90

Lev Shestov (Léon Chestov) did yeoman's work in trying to free European culture from the fetters of scientism. But he went astray in attempting to demolish *rationality* per se, the rationality that was at the heart of all his own writings. He subordinated his mind to the Judeo-Christian Bible, to the irrational "God of Abraham, Isaac, and Jacob." Perhaps he was influenced by Heine whom he admired, who had done the same, but only when he was in the grip of a paralytic illness. It was left to a man of letters, D. H. Lawrence, in an introduction to a collection of Shestov's earlier essays (*All Things Are Possible*, 1920), to state the real consequences of Shestov's thought: "Let each individual act spontaneously from the forever-incalculable promptings of the well-head within him. There is no universal law. Each being is, at his purest, a law unto himself, single, unique, a Godhead, a fountain from the unknown." This is not nihilism. This is, as Lawrence stated himself, only a "shaking free" of the human soul from the bonds of religious or scientific dogmatism.

Too bad that Lawrence's words have not had an impact on contemporary religion or philosophy.

91

At times I wonder whether I have done right in becoming a recluse and absenting myself from the stimuli and pleasures of societal living. But then I remember the greater pleasure of being my own man and feeling my soul expand. One of the greatest virtues in living amidst nature is the absence of the noise and pressures of urbanized existence—and almost all living in America today is "urbanized." Thus I can more readily experience the metaphysical realities that exist behind the physical world. Solitude is always available and solitude is the *sine qua non* of finding the God within oneself.

Without metaphysical awareness, nature becomes mere scenery. Experiencing it is then no different than watching movies or looking at picture postcards.

* * *

I feel it necessary to admit that lack of recognition of *who I am* by the outer world often produces a sense of discomfort in me, at times verging on *angst*. I see this as analogous to the visceral sensation of hunger or the psychological one of fear. It stems from the herd instinct of many animal species that exists in me in a residual form. I haven't been able to extirpate it completely but recognizing its nature is quite helpful for my state of mind. I remind myself that only the person who can live alone, psychologically as well as physically, is truly a free person.

92

I feel myself to be primarily a metaphysical being and therefore metaphysical experience is the most fulfilling for me. I am no longer interested in any writings that are not existential, i.e. reflective of the soul of the writer. This eliminates virtually all of contemporary philosophy from my sphere of interest. Nor is there any connection for me with the Abrahamic religions. In my judgment, Ralph Waldo Emerson is the closest thing to a spiritual "savior" that one can find in Western letters. It is his writings and not the superannuated testaments of millennia ago that should be studied, restudied, and studied again.

* * *

I find that the intermediate state between sleep and wakefulness is the one in which I am most likely to become conscious of the metaphysical dimension of my existence. This is probably because as soon as I leave my bed, the distractions of the material world bear down heavily upon me. Like Gresham's law that bad money drives out good, the material world drives out metaphysical consciousness. The latter is like a delicate orchid requiring optimum conditions to flourish. But the material world is transitory, whereas the metaphysical is eternal. Deep experiences I have had never leave my mind as opposed to superficial material ones, which are like leaves blowing in the wind. The most significant experience I have ever had is finding

God in my own soul. This experience is permanently imprinted within me.

93

Emerson said of Theodore Parker (1810–1860) that he was the Savonarola of New England. Our era is even more in need of a Savonarola than was Parker's. We need a similarly strong, incorruptible personality to cleanse away the vast corruptions of America. I fear, however, that the task would be beyond human capabilities and one day, instead of the humane Savonarola, we might get a Robespierre or a Lenin.

* * *

The domineering policy of my country in the world is an embarrassment to me. The United States government throws its weight around everywhere and into everything. Fortunately, I no longer travel abroad where I would be ashamed to admit I am an American. All empires historically have come to end and I can't see where the American empire stretching from the Atlantic to the Pacific will be any exception. Most people I have encountered are unhappy with their government and pessimistic about it. All that is needed is the economy to worsen and a lighted match to start a conflagration. But I don't think it will happen in my lifetime. *Après moi, le déluge.*

* * *

Sometimes I like to engage in geopolitical ruminations. When the American empire (and Canada) breaks up, I imagine the northern half of the Atlantic seaboard becoming independent, the *United Atlantic States*. The Maritime Provinces of Canada would join them when *Quebec* achieves its long desired independence. New York City might secede to become a new Singapore. The South would rise again as an independent *New Confederacy*, freed from the problem of slavery. *Texas*, no longer under threat from Mexico, would again become an independent country. The hispanicized Southwest would become *Anglo-Hispanic America,* unconnected to Mexico. California would probably split in half—the south joining *Anglo-Hispanic America*, the north joining a new northwest *Pacific America*, including British Columbia, Yukon, and Alaska. The heart of The United States, middle America, would probably merge with its correlative Canadian areas to form a vast new nation, *Middle America*, with a relatively homogeneous North American culture whose frontier might be the Northwest Territories of Canada.

These are all fantasies of course. But many more fantastic things have occurred throughout history.

94

The other day Gustavo visited me again. He said he had a big favor to ask of me. He wants to cross over to the United States with his family. His arthritis is getting worse and he feels he can no longer transport marijuana across the border. He has a relative in Tucson who is willing to help him. Gustavo had a plan all figured out, but it needed my cooperation. He will cross with his whole family on foot on a night with a full moon so as to have maximum visibility. Initially he will reach my cabin where they would need to rest for a few hours before proceeding on foot for about 15 miles more. A truck would meet them well off the highway. Hopefully, their contact would know about the checkpoint on the road north to Tucson. "Please Señor," Gustavo pleaded, "I need a little help from you. I can't live in Mexico anymore."

What could I say? I didn't like participating in illegal immigration but I felt I couldn't refuse. A few days later, Gustavo, his wife, son, daughter, and two-year-old granddaughter showed up at my cabin in the evening. The family didn't say much but the child cried continuously in spite of the mother's efforts to pacify it. I gave each a beer and a sandwich I had purchased for them earlier, and $20 to Gustavo. He kept thanking me profusely, which made me even more uncomfortable for I felt I should have been doing more for them. Toward midnight, they gathered their things and took off single file on an old dirt road near the cabin. It was a pathetic sight. I will probably never know whether they reached their destination safely.

The incomprehensibility of the destiny of individual human beings is a distressing reality. Conflict and catastrophe are everywhere. My kind of life was as irrelevant to Gustavo as to the animals of the forest. Yet I suppose everyone must play out the cards that are dealt to them, I with my solitary metaphysical thinking under comfortable circumstances and Gustavo with making a new life for his family under insecure conditions in the United States. Somehow there should be some sense to it all, an explanation for everything. But I haven't been able to find any such.

95

I have been plodding through Alexander Solzhenitsyn's immense novel *August 1914.* It is the story of Russia's early catastrophic defeat during World War I. It has some personal interest for me because the site of much of the activity is not far from my ancestral origins. Solzhenitsyn describes in painful detail the incompetency and failures of the Russian general staff. About three quarters through the novel, there appears this unexpected exchange between the student Sanya and a wise old man Varsonofiev. Sanya has asked if it is possible to develop an "ideal social order." Varsonofiev responds: "The word 'develop' has a better and more important application—we should develop our *soul.* There is nothing more precious than the development of a man's own soul; it is more important than the well-being of countless future generations" [Solzhenitsyn, A.: *August 1914,* Bantam Books, p. 473, trans. Michael Glenny–Ed.].

This is the most important thought in the entire novel, but it is wedged within the substance of a long, intricate, historical account. The idea is not developed further. This is often the fate of philosophical insights inserted into novels; they are lost amidst the more diverting appeal of the story. Yet Solzhenitsyn deserves high honor for expressing the thought at all. One cannot imagine finding such a thought in an English-language novel.

96

A shadow lies over the land in which I live. It is that of the Apache Indians who lived here for centuries before the intrusion of Americans. They had worked out a *modus vivendi* with the Spaniards during the colonial period but this ended with Mexican independence. The fierce Apaches were generally successful in keeping Mexicans out of their lands but it all changed when the Americans with their army arrived, following their

Manifest Destiny. After the longest war in American history, Geronimo finally surrendered and all Apaches were transported to distant reservations. Those who didn't go were hunted down and killed. It was the end of Apache history in southern Arizona. *Vae victis,* as some Roman once said. Adding insult to injury, Cochise County in the southeastern part of the state is named after the Apache chieftain who had been most successful in resisting American occupation of Apache lands.

Sometimes I see ghostly figures on horseback dashing over the grasslands or slinking through the forests. I can't see them clearly but I think they are Apaches trying to return to their homeland. Of course they are figments of my imagination, but then again, who knows what the future might bring. The Anglo civilization has been here less time than was the case with the Apaches. A civilization in which I guiltily feel I share.

97

I have always felt that I have two personas: one a mask that I wore in my working life—superficially friendly, intellectual, undemanding. It is a mask I put on in the company of people. The other persona is my usual one at the present time—reclusive, mystical, dwelling in the atmosphere of a metaphysical consciousness.

However, now I have discovered a third unexpected persona of mine, a Caliban figure (Shakespeare, *The Tempest*) whose hand is raised against the world—paranoid, hostile, and aggressive, especially sexually, a genuinely monster-like persona. This one emerges at night in my dreams, but sometimes carries over into my waking hours. I really don't know what to make of this bizarre Caliban and at times he frightens me. I fervently hope in an afterlife he will be gone.

Most of the time I live in a mental world quite remote from the one around me. Both may be "real" but exist at differing levels of reality. It is to be expected that I prefer my own level.

* * *

If the metaphysical "beyond" in which I have put my faith truly exists, the management of my life has been correct. If not, and my entire being molders in a material grave after death, I will have no awareness of this fact and will have lost nothing except having dispensed with the dubious joys of social intercourse during the last half of my life. Thus my attitude is a win-win one.

This thought may be reminiscent of Pascal's wager mentioned above. I have always considered his calculating weighing of pluses and minuses in choosing a faith was not worthy of a philosopher. But I am clear that my choice has been based on an inner compulsion, not the totting up of pros and cons of available possibilities.

98

When I was young (it seems so long ago), I was mad for new experiences: people, travel, danger, relationships. These experiences were needful to me then. But now I have learned that the greatest experience of all is the experience of metaphysical reality. For that I only need leisure, solitude, my library, and my writing tools.

* * *

Looking over this journal, it seems to me to be more akin to a gigantic medieval tapestry than to a literary narrative. Who could examine every detail? Who would want to? Fortunately, I have no expectations in this regard. The journal has served its purpose for me.

99

The concept that all philosophy is basically a preparation for death is an old idea that stretches back to antiquity. I do not know who might have first enunciated it. For a long time, I did not really understand the concept. It could not merely refer to arranging one's affairs, preparing a will, or stating beneficiaries. All these would be unworthy of philosophic thought. But now I think I understand its meaning. It refers to preparing one's soul for crossing the great divide called death. The soul needs to be prepared for what comes to it upon passing over to the other side. This means preparing it for a metaphysical existence that will participate in the ultimate metaphysical reality. The more one creates metaphysical awareness during his lifetime, the more he will be able to contribute to this reality. The language I use here will hardly do justice to my intuition but it is the best I can do. I have been slow to apprehend metaphysical reality and have been fortunate to have had a long life in which to do so.

It has been often said that the awareness of metaphysical reality is *ineffable*, meaning that it is beyond human description. However, ineffability is hardly limited to metaphysical phenomena. All forms of sensory perception are ineffable in that the perceptions cannot be described by language (or other human forms of communication). The sensation of the color "yellow" cannot be communicated through language and is only meaningful to those who have experienced the color yellow themselves. The same is true of all forms of perception. One has to have a prior experience of the sensation being communicated in order for a linguistic symbol to be meaningful. It is an old axiom that the experiences of sight cannot be communicated to one who has been blind from birth.

The same is true of metaphysical experiences. Thus the real

depth of meaning of the symbol "God" cannot be grasped by those who have not themselves had metaphysical experiences. In fact, metaphysical experience is rare and hard to achieve in this life. One's soul must be prepared and the intellect capable of understanding metaphysical reality. The domain of metaphysics is beyond life and it may be that merely traces of it can be found in one's lifetime. The great mystics of history have only had occasional metaphysical (mystical) experiences during their lives. Plotinus, perhaps the greatest mystic of all times, said of himself that he experienced the fullness of God only four times. Today in the atmosphere of scientism, it is virtually impossible for individuals educated in this atmosphere to experience metaphysical reality. The effort, however, needs to be made.

100

My own self is still a mystery to me. Methinks there are no clear answers to the human enigma. Perhaps that is as it should be. But we humans don't think sufficiently highly of ourselves as spiritual individuals. In a concept of the cosmic scheme of things, we as individuals must be more, God must be not as much—and our "society" must be least of all. The last ought to be firmly put in its place by all right-minded persons.

Garrulousness in the form of rhetoric, erudition, or other types of verbosity is a vice that should be avoided by independent philosophers. I think I am as guilty of it as any other. It is very difficult to overcome the world with words. *Est-ce que je suis un "philosophe maudit"?* I fear I might commit spiritual suicide as did poor Nietzsche. I couldn't stand requiring an attendant.

* * *

[Here Landesman's journal came to an abrupt end as if the writer could write no more. I had considered deleting the last paragraph of the last segment, which seemed incongruent with the rest of the journal and might indicate the beginnings of some kind of nervous breakdown. Finally, I decided that it too reflected Landesman's soul and left it in place. —Ed.]

* * *

BIOBIBLIOGRAPHY WITH NAME INDEX

A

B

C

D

E

G

H

J

K

L

M

N

P

PASCAL, Blaise (1623-1662) French literary great; composed *Pensées,* one of the first examples of religious existentialist writing; 50, 167

PENFIELD, Wilder (1891-1976) Pioneer Canadian neurosurgeon; student of Sherrington *(The Mystery of the Mind);* 64

PESSOA, Fernando (1888-1935) Portuguese poet and original prose writer; national culture figure of Portugal *(Livro do Desassossego);* xi, 92

PETRARCH (1304-1374) Italian poet and forerunner of Renaissance humanism *(Il Mio Segreto);* 14, 77, 109, 111, 144, 156, 157

PLATO (427 B.C.-347 B.C.) Towering founder of western philosophy; strong metaphysical orientation *(Phaedo; Timaeus);* 34, 61, 67, 88, 95, 121, 132, 133, 134, 141, 156, 157

PLOTINUS (204-270) Influential Roman mystical philosopher, non-Christian; generally regarded as originator of neoplatonism in philosophy *(Enneads);* 170

R

ROSENZWEIG, Franz (1886-1929) German-Jewish religious philosopher *(Stern der Erlösung);* ix

RUSSELL, Lord Bertrand (1872-1970) British philosopher, mathematician, and radical social critic *(Why I Am Not A Christian);* 81, 90, 100

S

SARTRE, Jean-Paul (1905-1980) Dean of French existentialism; playwright, novelist, political activist; refused Nobel Prize *(L'existentialisme est un humanisme);* 84

SAVONAROLA, Girolamo (1452-1498) Italian priest and theologian; forerunner of Martin Luther; burnt on a stake in Florence (Martines: *Fire in the City*); 148, 161

T

U

V

W

X

ABOUT THE AUTHOR

RICHARD SCHAIN obtained A.B. (philosophy) and M.D. degrees from New York University. He trained in neurology at the Yale Medical Center, later serving as professor of neurology and psychiatry at UCLA. He embarked on his life as an independent philosopher in 1980 to pursue philosophical writings on the significance of the interior self, the soul. Schain thinks of Leon Landesman as his alter ego.

Schain's book, *Toward an Existential Philosophy of the Soul* (2014), received *Foreword Reviews* 2014 INDIEFAB Book of the Year Silver Award for Philosophy. His other books include:

Affirmations of Reality (1982)
Philosophical Artwork (1983)
Souls Exist (1989, 2013)
The Legend of Nietzsche's Syphilis (2001)
Reverence for the Soul (2001)
Radical Metaphysics (2002)
Behold the Philosopher (2007)
Interior Lights (2012).